DISCARD

P9-CBX-873

Pieces fRom LIfe's Crazy QuiLt

Marvin V. Arnett

University of Nebraska Press

Lincoln and London

JEFFERSON PUBLIC LIBRARY
321 S. Main Street
Jefferson, WI 53549
·674-7733

© 2000, 2003 Marvin V. Arnett
All rights reserved
Manufactured in the
United States of America
♾
Library of Congress
Cataloging-in-Publication Data
Arnett, Marvin V., 1928–
Pieces from life's crazy quilt / Marvin V. Arnett.
p. cm. — (American lives)
ISBN 0-8032-1064-7 (cl.: alk. paper)
1. Arnett, Marvin V., 1928—Childhood and youth.
2. African Americans—Michigan—Detroit—Biography.
3. Detroit (Mich.)—Biography. I. Title. II. Series.
F574.D49 N424 2003
977.4'3400496073'0092—dc21
[B]
2002029135

JEFFERSON PUBLIC LIBRARY
321 S. Main Street
Jefferson, WI 53549
574-7735

CONTENTS

Acknowledgments

All honor to my Lord and Savior Jesus Christ, who makes all things possible; Professor Bill Linn, associate professor of English language and literature, Humanities Department, University of Michigan–Dearborn, without whom there would be no book; Professor Jackie Lawson, associate professor of English language and literature, Humanities Department, University of Michigan–Dearborn, for her encouragement and support; Julius E. Thompson, PhD, director, Black Studies Program, University of Missouri–Columbia, who took time to review and advise; Michael Steinberg, editor, Fourth Genre: Explorations in Nonfiction, generous to a fault; Thelma Acty, Peggy Castine, Telytha Mullins, who were there in the beginning; and to True Believers everywhere.

Pieces from Life's Crazy Quilt

Prologue

In the 1920s, Detroit, Michigan, was a city on the move. The rapidly expanding automobile industry drew people from all over the nation. Every day, throngs of southern migrants, black and white, swelled the city's population. They came in search of higher wages and a better way of life and found a highly industrialized city that had managed to retain its small-town atmosphere.

The summer of 1928 was long and hot. Belle Isle beaches were dense with people attempting to beat the heat. In the poorer neighborhoods, firemen opened fire hydrants to cool children who did not have access to the waterfront. Icemen struggled to meet the demand for ice, while peddlers hawked "sweet, ripe watermelons" from horse-drawn wagons. At neighborhood parks, the primal call to "play ball" was heard far into the evening. It was no wonder that Negroes arriving from the south considered Detroit the Promised Land.

In 1928 the use of "Negro" was status quo—it wasn't until many years later that this name, and "Colored," were rejected and replaced by "African-American" or "black." A shortage of housing was also the status quo in 1928 Detroit. And what housing the new arrivals found available was sub-standard. Structures that in white neighborhoods would have been torn down were rented to blacks at highly inflated rates. Vermin often infiltrated their neighborhoods, and constant effort was required to maintain a semblance of cleanliness and order.

The majority of Detroit's black population lived in an area known as Black Bottom, located on the east side of the city, not far from the Detroit River. On the west side, enclaves of blacks developed, surrounded by their white counterparts. These areas became self-contained cities within the city. Outside their boundaries, blacks met with overwhelming racial prejudice and animosity and thus would usually leave their neighborhood only to go to and from their jobs. Inside their boundaries, whites operated businesses designed to provide the basic needs of the residents. Only the black church stood as a beacon of hope in an otherwise bleak landscape.

Since faith was the one thing the white man could not take away, the Negro held on to it with fierce determination. No matter how difficult the workweek, no matter how small the paycheck, Sunday morning would find most residents giving their presence and financial support to a place of worship. It was in church that you could figuratively lay your troubles at the "throne of grace" and return to the battlefield the following Monday, secure in the knowledge that all would be well. After all, the Lord had not brought you this far to forsake you!

For those with more worldly inclinations, there were always the midnight-to-dawn dances at the Graystone Ballroom, the cafés, shops, and food vendors along St. Antoine Street, and the rent parties that blossomed every weekend.

While church and nightlife combined to make life bearable for blacks in Detroit, it was the hopes and dreams for their children that kept them pressing forward. Higher education was considered the road to success in life. Though it was true that many college graduates were unable to find jobs in their chosen field, most parents clung to the opinion that things would eventually get better and that the person with a college education would be ready to take advantage of the change when it came.

Late in 1928, an event occurred that challenged the validity of that belief. The Ford Motor Company closed all of its manufacturing plants and ended production of the Model T car. In most history books, the Great Depression is listed as officially beginning in 1930, but the closing of the Ford plants was the financial death knell for the city of Detroit.

It was into this rapidly deteriorating world that Marvin Verona Sprague was born on the eighth day of July in the year 1928 at Herman Kiefer Hospital in Detroit, Michigan. Although born poor, black, and female, she did have the good fortune to be born William Sprague's daughter and Grace Melissa's child. In the end, that was enough.

MY MOTHER'S QUILTS

henever I dream of my mother, she is always sitting at the dining room table, sorting through an endless array of quilt scraps.

My mother had many gifts. She made lighter-than-air angel food cakes using bacon drippings for shortening. The aroma of her freshly baked bread stopped grown men in their tracks. With only a glance at a designer fashion, she could duplicate it to the last exquisite detail. She designed and crocheted prize-winning lace tablecloths and bedspreads. She fashioned from used garments outfits for her children that rivaled clothing sold in the best children's boutiques. She worshipped her God. But above and beyond all, she made quilts.

For my mother, quilt making took the place of the many vanities practiced by most women. Fashion and glamour meant nothing to her. She saved her true artistic gifts for making quilts. She designed quilts in every design and color, size and pattern: practical quilts designed to provide warmth; elaborately patterned quilts designed to show off her quilt making skills; and baby quilts designed from white squares adorned with embroidered kittens and puppies, lollipops and teddy bears. I cannot remember a time when my mother's quilts were not a major part of our lives.

While my mother pieced all styles of quilts, her favorite was the crazy quilt— a quilt that could as easily decorate a wall as cover a bed. She said it was named crazy quilt because it didn't follow a set pattern. It was left to the individual quilt maker to develop a random pattern.

My mother's quilts were random, both in design and material. An uneven scrap left over from a pair of my brother's wool pants was attached to a scrap from my sister's white satin baby bonnet. Gingham scraps from discarded aprons were married to red velvet scraps from an old bathrobe. Brightly colored silk and satin ribbons were used to highlight the almost oriental patterns of the quilts. The quilts were also heavily embroidered and often covered with tiny crocheted replicas of butterflies, blue birds, and flags, or any item that caught Mother's fancy. The images of my mother's beautiful quilts haunt me to this day.

It was during the long winter evenings my mother spent sorting through her quilt scraps that I asked her questions, piecing together the segments of my family history. As a member of my family's second generation to be born outside of slavery, this record was, of necessity, brief.

Father was the youngest of fourteen children, and all the members of his family, with the exception of his half brother, Smitty, were dead and buried long before I came into this world—at least all of the brothers and sisters that he knew about. It seemed that Grandpa Sprague was a legend in his hometown. Father said it was anybody's guess how many illegitimate children he had fathered during his lifetime. I do know that my father was born in Greenville, Tennessee, and left home at the age of fifteen, never to return.

My mother's family was a different story. I knew Grandpa Elisha and Grandma Alice because they came to visit several times. They were much older than my friends' grandparents and both had been born into slavery. Grandma Alice remembered her uncle coming into the yard one day and throwing her up in the air while shouting, "Lincoln freed the slaves! Lincoln freed the slaves!"

Grandpa Elisha's background was unique for his time. The only son of a wealthy tobacco farmer and a female slave, he had been given unusual opportunities to learn and grow. He attended a small school on the outskirts of Louisville, Kentucky. Of course, he was not officially enrolled but was hired as a janitor and allowed to sit at the rear of the room and listen to the lessons. There was grumbling among the students' parents, but since his father was the wealthiest landowner in the county, my grandfather was allowed to stay. When he married, his father deeded him a parcel of land just outside the small town of Berry, Kentucky. It was there in a three-room farmhouse that my mother and her sister were born and raised.

During the 1920s and 1930s the federal government instituted a project to reduce illiteracy among the hill people. When they attempted to send a white teacher to the Moonlight School, the hill people ran him off. They insisted that the only teacher they would accept would be my grandfather. He had befriended many of the adults by writing responses to the letters they received from their children who had traveled up north to find fame and fortune. My grandmother would tell of the soft tapping at their back door late at night. There would stand one of the hill people with a rumpled envelope clutched, tightly, in their hands.

No matter how late the hour, Grandfather would read the letter aloud several times and patiently write the response dictated to him. Grandmother would graciously accept the jar of pickles or jelly offered as a token of thanks, and the visitor would slip, quietly, out the back door.

After several failed attempts to force white teachers on the hill people, the government reluctantly capitulated but insisted on paying Grandfather in cash while maintaining no paper trail of the transaction.

Against this jumbled background, it is a mystery how my father, who had worked as a bartender, chef, carpenter, and who had sung in the chorus of an opera company while working abroad as a chauffeur, and my mother, a woman who had lived in only three places in her entire life, met, married, and remained together until parted by death. But mystery or not, they did.

IN MY FATHER'S HOUSE

In the fall of 1932, our family moved into a house on Herbert Street in Detroit, Michigan. The family consisted of my father, mother, brother, sister, and me. I was the baby, an unanticipated birth that happened when both parental energies and the national economy were at low ebb. I was born in 1928 on the east side of Detroit. Nineteen twenty-eight was not a banner year for any American to be born, much less any Negro American. I would grow up during the Great Depression in a racially mixed neighborhood on the west side of the city in a house referred to by one and all as the Green House. There I would experience the racial prejudice that was the automatic byproduct of my black skin.

The name Green House did not refer to plants and flowers but to the building's nauseous, bile green color. The federal government had flooded the market with large quantities of surplus green paint priced at only ten cents a gallon—first come, first served. According to Mr. Holts, owner of the neighborhood hardware store, landlords of rental properties in predominately black neighborhoods snapped up the entire quantity in less than two days.

Why our building was identified by its color, instead of by its address, remained a mystery since many other rental properties on the street were painted the same color. Perhaps it was because it was the only wooden multiple-family dwelling on the block. When my father, with his customary flair for being a touch different, painted the steps, porches, and supporting columns of both the upper and lower flats with black lacquer paint, the green paint appeared even greener. Whatever the reason, the Green House it was, and the Green House it remained until it was torn down in 1962.

Before moving to the Green House, our family shared a four-room apartment on the east side with an acquaintance of my father. He was a nice enough fellow, but, in reality, he was looking for someone to cook his meals and keep the place clean. My mother more than filled the bill. Housing for families with children was difficult to find, so she patiently put up with the inconvenience.

When both Aunt Bessie and Uncle Smitty moved to the west side of town, Mother's mood changed. Not even constant visits to her church, just around the corner on St. Antoine Street, raised her spirits. She became so despondent that when my uncle mentioned the vacant flat on Herbert Street, my father rushed to rent it, sight unseen.

The flat was shabby, even by rental standards, but it was in an ideal location; Aunt Bessie lived only a block and a half away on Bangor Street, and Uncle Smitty lived less than a block away on Scotten Avenue. So, Father struck a bargain with the landlord—in exchange for enough paint and wallpaper to redecorate the flat, he would perform minor repairs around the building. Mr. Guntz, our landlord, was in constant trouble with the City of Detroit Housing Authority. He welcomed a chance to get some of his code violations corrected at little or no cost. It turned out that he had a brother who owned a dime store on Warren Avenue and sold premier paint and wallpaper seconds at a fraction of their original cost. Father said, "If I had known that, I would have driven a harder bargain."

Like most of the houses in predominantly Polish neighborhoods, the rooms in the flat were designed more for entertaining than for living. While the living and dining rooms were mammoth and the kitchen adequate, the bedrooms were little more than alcoves. The only door in the flat, other than the front and back doors, was the bathroom door. All other rooms had archways hung with drapes in place of doors. One of the first things Father did was to replace the drapes to his bedroom with a wooden door scrounged from the salvage yard on Michigan Avenue.

Mother busied herself with the massive task of scrubbing and cleaning. Floors were scoured with a caustic soap-and-bleach concoction that left her hands pasty white and deeply wrinkled. True to his word, the landlord provided enough wallpaper and pungent-smelling paint to refurbish the flat. My parents split the work: Father did the painting, and Mother did the wallpapering. And Mr. Howell, who worked for a construction company, brought some linseed oil to cut the odor. It seemed to help, although Uncle Smitty said it really didn't reduce the odor, we just got used to it.

Mother's wallpapering was a work of art. She would spend hours hanging and re-hanging strips of wallpaper, determined to obtain a perfect pattern match. When she finished, you couldn't tell where the seams of the strips met.

At last, the work was completed. Mother called us to her and said, "We're making a fresh start. We've got a clean home, and we're going to keep it that way. I want you children to promise to do your part to keep this place spick-and-span. You don't want to live in a pig sty, do you?"

While we assured my mother over and over again that we would do everything possible to keep our house clean, Aunt Bessie sat at the kitchen table shaking her head in disbelief. "Gracie," she said, "I see you have a lot to learn about living in a four-family flat. Keeping a clean house has little to do with how often you clean and a lot to do with how often your neighbors clean."

It didn't take long to understand what Aunt Bessie meant. Common walls of the building were paper thin. It was an old building in a poor state of repair. Several rooms had large cracks in the walls, which Father attempted to repair, but the plaster patch would not hold. Mother's beautiful crazy quilts proved the perfect cover-up for the flawed walls. The floors were warped, and the molding separated from the walls in several places. The result was a building where if one flat had cockroaches, they all did.

One of the largest selling items at the corner grocery store was something called the roach bomb. It was a pressurized metal cylinder filled with a powerful chemical bug killer. Once all windows and doors were closed, and all cracks and crevices stuffed with rags, the bomb was placed in a central room and the pin pulled. Immediately, a chemical would spray from the bomb filling the air with a thick cloud of insecticide that quickly invaded every nook and cranny of the flat. The person setting the bomb would exit the premises immediately after pulling the pin and not return for at least eight hours.

At the end of the eight-hour period, the flat would be unsealed, and the cleanup began. Everything in the flat had to be scrubbed down with Fels Naphtha Soap and bleach. The odors generated by combining these two products required airing the flat out for several additional hours. That night, we would sleep in our roach-free home with smiles on our faces.

There was only one problem. It was impossible to get all the tenants to wage war at the same time. Without a unified battle plan, the cockroaches would regroup and conduct attack after attack until rebuked by the next bombing.

Mother never gave up the fight. One day, when purchasing a roach bomb from the clerk at Davison Grocery Store, she mentioned how hard she fought to get rid of roaches only to have them flood back from the adjacent flat. In exasperation, she said, "I don't know why the Lord burdened colored folks with roaches. You would think we had enough to bear."

She was surprised when the clerk replied, "Miss Grace, you don't really believe that it's only colored folks who have to fight roaches? Ask some of the ladies that do day work how many roach bombs they see in the white folks' trash. They just don't talk about it."

For many years my mother fought the battle in the firm belief that the good Lord didn't put any more on you than you could bear—that no matter how difficult the circumstances, he always provided a way out. She saw her sewing skills as our way out. As faithfully as she tithed money for the church, she tithed for a home of our own. She longed for an environment she could totally control without interference from anyone. Father would look at her in awe and say, "With that much faith, God wouldn't dare disappoint you."

The neighborhood we moved into was more like a small village than a loose collection of streets. Within a twenty-mile radius was everything needed to live the good life, except the funds required. While whites owned most of the businesses, the owners knew that their profits, or lack thereof, rested solely on the shoulders of the Negro customers who frequented their stores. By shopping within the boundaries of the neighborhood, we were spared the obligatory rudeness directed toward us by the white clerks who staffed the downtown stores. This proved a mixed blessing as neighborhood storeowners were free to set exorbitant prices since few people in the area owned cars.

The sense of village was also reflected in the responsibility felt by adults toward the care and feeding of all the neighborhood children. I soon learned that this, too, was a mixed blessing. Adults within a ten-block radius thought it was their God-given responsibility to act in loco parentis if the need arose. Since no two seemed to agree on what was right and proper, it made for some interesting dialogues.

"Marvin Sprague, what do you mean walking around bareheaded? You'll get sunstroke! Put that babushka on your head before I tell your father what you're up to! I thought you had more sense than that!"

"Yes, Mrs. Killum."

"Maude, leave that child alone. She's got sense enough to know if she's too warm. Grown folks should quit picking on children. They make good children bad. Marvin, if that babushka makes you too warm, take it off!"

"Yes, Mr. Killum."

If you're wondering why the titles sir and ma'am were missing, it was because my father had this strange notion that such titles were to be earned, not given.

According to some in the neighborhood, this was not the only strange notion he held. New arrivals in the area were immediately warned that Mr. Sprague took a dim view of anyone striking one of his children. Under certain circumstances, it might be permissible to verbally chastise them, but the laying on of hands was strictly forbidden. This warning was taken seriously, as it was believed that any man who would name his daughter Marvin was capable of just about anything. My father's stand on corporal punishment led many of the elders in the neighborhood to prophesy a lifetime of heartache for my parents. They held the strong belief that to spare the rod was to spoil the child.

When Mother learned that the small storefront church located on the first floor of our building was an offshoot of her previous church home, she joined immediately. In time, her devotion to the church spun a security blanket over my father and his strange ways. It was thought that there must be some good in him or else why would a sweet, gentle woman like my mother have married him. Our father countered by saying that the church sister's laudatory comments seemed to increase in direct proportion to the number of crocheted altar clothes and seat covers my mother made for the church sanctuary.

While Mother toiled at forging a strong relationship with members of the Church of the True Believers, Father was accepted into the male hierarchy with open arms. His fame had preceded him. Uncle Smitty had many friends in the area, and he did not hesitate to regale them with stories of the travels and exploits of his half brother, Bill. Since the travel experience of most of the men was limited to their passage from various southern states to the Promised Land up north, they were duly impressed. My father did not have to prove himself. He only had to not prove Uncle Smitty a liar.

As for my brother, he drifted through the move with his usual calm assurance. There were a few attempts by some of the teenage boys to test that assurance, but they met with complete failure. He was grudgingly accepted into the neighborhood circle. After all, it's a little difficult to harass a ten-year-old boy who stands five feet six inches tall and weighs 165 pounds. Mother said, "God made William tall and strong to protect him from bullies. With his quiet, studious nature, he would make the perfect victim."

My sister, Jewel, seldom lifted her head from her precious Bible scrapbooks. As long as she could attend church, Sunday school, and play Bible school at home, nothing else seemed to matter. She carried her magic with her. From the moment we moved in, everyone in the neighborhood, black and white, young and old, fell completely and hopelessly in love with her. It was her mission in life to be loved.

My entrance into the neighborhood was a quiet affair. As a four-year-old housebound "baby," I was completely ignored by the neighborhood children. Only my beloved Jewel would take time to play with me. My mother dried my tears by reminding me that in only one more year, I would enter kindergarten and become a big kid too.

Summer came, and gradually the image of the Green House changed. It didn't change physically, although Father did shore up the wobbly porch rail that circled the L-shaped porch with two-by-fours and built screen doors from scrap lumber and screening salvaged from broken window screens he found in the alley. It didn't change in the eyes of our neighbors, who continued to refer to it as the Green House. It changed in the minds and hearts of the members of my family. It was the experiences we shared while living in the Green House that changed the way we viewed it. Good, bad, or indifferent, they led to our recognition of the Green House as more than just a building. It became our home.

THE JEWEL IN THE CROWN

My world was one of ever-changing parameters. Each succeeding year expanded both its physical and emotional boundaries until eventually they extended to the edges of the four continents and to the capacity of the human heart. But that state was reached many decades later.

In the beginning of memory, the boundaries were limited to the distance between my hands and the hem of my mother's dress. By the age of four, they had stretched to the five rooms that comprised our flat and the attached L-shaped porch. By the time I entered kindergarten, they included the backyard and the sidewalk in front of our building. Within this space, many a life and death drama was played out. But none more tragic than the loss of my sister, the "Jewel in our Crown."

Since William was ten years old when Jewel died, and I was only five, much of what I learned about her death was related to me by my brother. Although his knowledge of the facts surrounding Jewel's death was far better than mine, from a vantage point deep within my heart, dim images emerged that helped to fill the gaps in his story.

Like most tragic stories, it began at a point filled with light. It was June 1933. School was out, and vacation Bible school had yet to begin. A golden time! The only weeks of the summer vacation that belonged utterly and completely to the neighborhood children. Since I would not attend kindergarten until the following September, my joy was tempered by a lack of understanding of how deeply my brother and sister valued the freedom of those days. As Mother's constant companion, every day was free to me. I did relish the fact that I now had my siblings available all day long to harass and annoy instead of just for a couple of hours in the evening.

Jewel convened her annual play school for which, as usual, there was no lack of students. To understand why every kid in the neighborhood—including boys at least twice her age—were more than willing, even eager, to participate in her play school, you would have had to know Jewel. She was the beloved "jewel" of the entire neighborhood. Her appeal was not limited solely to those who knew her. Even in the highly prejudicial world of the 1930s, it was not unusual for my mother, when accompanied by Jewel, to be stopped numerous times while both men and women, black and white, stooped to smilingly admire the beautiful little girl. She was that rare individual who looked uniquely like herself.

Many years later a cousin sent me a color photograph of my brother and sister taken when he was eight and she was six years old. Although the photo was taken with black-and-white film, the photographer had, as was the custom of the day, colored it using pastel water tints. There they stood; she in a pink-lace-trimmed, baby doll dress, a wide ribbon in her hair, and white lace stockings peeking from the tops of her three-button, high-top shoes. My brother, resplendent in a navy blue double-breasted suit worn with a white ruffled shirt, stood beside her with his left arm thrown protectively around her shoulder. With her creamed coffee complexion, dimpled cheeks, wide set blue-green eyes, and soft, curly black hair, she looked more like a beautiful cherub then the child of a poor working-class Negro family.

If Jewel held an attraction for people, that attraction was multiplied when it came to animals. When she joined us on the front porch on a summer evening, our stoop immediately became a gathering place for animals of all descriptions. Stray cats and mongrel dogs assembled from everywhere. They seemed content just to lay at her feet in wait for the occasional light caress she would bestow on each of them. When she would leave the porch to work on one of her Bible scrapbooks, they would immediately wander off.

Oddly enough, my brother and I did not resent the attention paid to Jewel. Somehow we knew that she was entitled to special treatment. A family friend, Mrs. Eubanks, summed it up best when she said, "I think God made a mistake when he allowed her to slip through. Why, she's one of his angels as sure as I'm sitting here. Jewel's just too good for this world."

Mother would mumble, "Don't say that, Annie," and quickly change the subject.

One Sunday afternoon, when Jewel joined us on the front porch, we spotted a newcomer among her usual cortege of animal friends. It was a large taffy-colored cat. She was different from the usual stray animal seen in the neighborhood. Sleek, well fed, and meticulously groomed, she was obviously a well-loved member of some family. Father said she was probably lost from one of the large houses on the boulevard. Night after night the cat reappeared, and night after night Jewel fed her a saucer of milk. Over time, everyone accepted her as Jewel's cat, and Father made a bed for her on the back porch. William and I voted to name her Taffy because of the color of her fur, but Jewel insisted on naming her Sunburst. So Sunburst it was, and we soon grew to think of her as a member of the family.

Fall came, and school resumed. On my first day of kindergarten, I met Beatrice, a kindred spirit, who was to become my best friend. Together we would seek adventure and find it in ways we could not have imagined.

As fall deepened, the mornings became crisp and cold. Frost formed on the tops of bushes and fences, and the sound of birds disappeared. One afternoon, when Jewel said it was getting too cold to leave Sunburst on the back porch, Father replied, "Cats have been living outside since the beginning of time. Why should it be any different with Sunburst?"

Despite his words, one tearful glance from Jewel resulted in his moving Sunburst's bed to a place inside the backdoor. Gradually, the bed eased its way back to the corner of Jewel's sleeping alcove, there to lose its occupant to the warm shelter of Jewel's arms. Each morning found Sunburst fast asleep on her shoulder.

Halloween came and went, and the Thanksgiving holiday loomed invitingly. Already Mother was sifting through the canned goods in the kitchen pantry to determine what she had on hand versus what she would need to prepare the high feast of the year. Not even our Christmas meal came close to the groaning board set forth for the Thanksgiving holiday. No matter how tight money was, Mother always came up with a varied assortment of entrees, side dishes, relishes, and homemade desserts. Topping off this cornucopia of culinary delights would be the ubiquitous freezer of peach ice cream, prepared from fruit Mother had canned in the early fall. Even Jewel would tear herself away from her scrapbooks long enough to compete for a lick from the freezer's dasher.

But this Thanksgiving something was different. While my brother and I badgered my mother in the kitchen—snatching finger licks of icing from the cakes cooling on the sideboard and fighting over who would get the batter-covered mixing bowl—Jewel remained in bed with the covers pulled over her head. Ever since the beginning of the school term, she had seemed to grow increasingly tired and listless. Jewel had always been the first up in the morning, but lately Mother had to call her two or three times each morning before she would slowly drag herself up. On Thanksgiving morning, when Mother finally went to prod her awake, she found Jewel lying, semi-comatose, in a sweat-soaked bed. I will never forget the sound of my mother's voice as she screamed over and over again.

The days that followed were a complete blur. Mother and Father disappeared for long periods of time. Aunt Bessie said they were at the hospital sitting with Jewel. She was in a deep coma caused by something called spinal meningitis. My parents left early in the morning and returned late at night. Some nights I would awake to the sound of someone crying, only to have my father come and pat my back while humming me back to sleep.

Nothing was going right. Everyone in the family had to be tested for meningitis. Sunburst had disappeared, and my brother and I could not find her anywhere. When my father came home one day and asked, "Where is that damn cat?" we knew something was very wrong.

Our aunt told us the doctors thought Jewel might have caught her illness from Sunburst. Aunt Bessie, ever the optimist, tried to cheer us up by saying, "Thank God your tests came back negative."

Every man in the neighborhood joined in the search for Sunburst but without success. Hope of ever finding her had faded when one of the Scott boys ran across her body in the narrow pathway between the Eubanks' and Loomis' houses. She had been shot. The lab technicians at Receiving Hospital said her body was so riddled with bullets that it was impossible to test it for the meningitis virus. Neither the Eubanks or Loomis families reported hearing gunshots, so the matter was dropped. Then, one afternoon in mid-December, my parents returned from the hospital early, and all conjecture ended. My sister, Jewel—beautiful Jewel—had died.

While my mother spent the days following the funeral locked in her bedroom with only an occasional sob to prove she was still alive, my father spent long hours consoling my brother and me. Only his unusual silences and bloodshot eyes told the story of the deep pain he felt. One day, nearly two weeks after Jewel's funeral, my brother overheard Father say, "Bessie, this has gone on long enough. What must the children be thinking?"

Our aunt sighed and said, "I know. Let me talk to her."

Later that evening Aunt Bessie went into the bedroom and closed the door behind her. As hard as we strained to hear, we heard nothing. Father sat at the dining room table holding his head in his hands. Finally, after what seemed like an eternity, Aunt Bessie came out of the bedroom. She nodded to my father, gathered up her coat and hat, and left the house.

I don't believe my brother and I slept at all that night. When we finally did drop off, we awoke to the smell of bacon frying. When we peeked around the doorjamb, we saw Mother in the kitchen moving busily from stove to table to icebox, humming softly under her breath. When she spied us, she called out, "You children had better hurry and wash up before your food gets cold."

In unison we broke for the bathroom that annexed the back porch. As he pushed past me, my brother punched me in the side, slowing my progress just long enough for him to bolt ahead into the bathroom. A wave of hope swept over me. Perhaps in time our lives would return to normal. Perhaps in time all would again be right in our world. I turned toward the kitchen. I could still hear Mother humming her favorite hymn. As I rounded the corner and entered the kitchen, ripe with the aroma of brewing coffee, I shouted at the top of my lungs, "Mama! Mama! William hit me!"

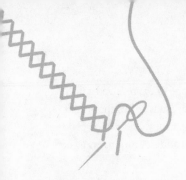

After the Fall

In the months that followed my sister's death, our family struggled to regain a sense of normalcy. The Christmas holiday followed so swiftly after the funeral that much of it seemed to trickle through the cracks of time. It is the Christmas I find difficult to remember. I am sure that Mother prepared the usual sumptuous midday feast. I faintly remember the artificial tree, lights shimmering, standing tall before the double windows in the living room. No doubt Father brought in the small workbench from the toolshed and placed it beside the tree to hold our few gifts. Perhaps I received coloring books and crayons or a box of Mary Jane paper dolls. I am sure I got a new wool scarf and gloves, for my mother knitted a new set each year. William would receive a science fiction magazine, a package of drafting paper, and a pack of assorted pencils. Our Christmas stockings were always filled with apples, oranges, and black walnuts, sent by our grandparents from Kentucky. The centerpiece of the holiday, however, was the gift packages delivered by the Goodfellows.

During my childhood, the Goodfellows, an organization of former newsboys who vowed that there would be no child without a Christmas in the Detroit metropolitan area, and the Salvation Army, who vowed to feed and cloth the hungry every day of the year, made our Christmas possible. Schools, churches, and social agencies began submitting the names of eligible children long before the Thanksgiving holiday. Local police officers served as couriers. They could be seen delivering gift packages as late as New Year's Day. In a city replete with racial prejudice, it was strange to see hard-boiled policemen cheerfully playing Santa to little Negro children. One officer in each precinct was assigned to Goodfellows's duty Christmas day so that church leaders, and interested citizens, could report the name and address of any child inadvertently overlooked.

Anticipation would be at fever pitch as children in the neighborhood awaited delivery of their Goodfellows's boxes. Girls, under the age of 12, received a doll, clothing, candy, and a certificate for a pair of shoes from Hudson's Department Store. Boys, under the age of 12, received a toy, clothing, candy, and a shoe certificate. After the age of 12, both sexes received a book, candy, clothing, and a certificate for a pair of shoes.

That year, as usual, the officer left three large boxes. Father stacked them in a corner of the living room until my mother returned from shopping. When she and Aunt Bessie returned, they realized immediately what had happened. We had received three boxes because no one had thought to have Jewel's name removed from the Goodfellows's list.

When Mother opened the box marked Jewel Sprague, she found the usual clothing along with a beautiful bride doll. Aunt Bessie looked at the doll and asked, "Gracie, isn't that the grand-prize winner pictured in the Detroit News last week?"

The most anticipated item in a young girl's Goodfellows's box was the doll. Volunteers dressed the dolls, and many wore elaborately crocheted and embroidered outfits. Each year, after Thanksgiving, they were displayed on a large platform in the lobby of the Detroit News building while a panel of judges selected the first-, second-, and third-prize winners in the doll-dressing competition. Although the Goodfellows stoutly maintained that the dolls were distributed randomly, it was an annual joke in our neighborhood that the only dolls we would see would be the ones dressed in cheap dime-store outfits. After we received the prize-winning doll, Aunt Bessie grudgingly admitted, "I guess we'll just have to eat those words."

The doll was an instant sensation. People came from as far away as Milford Avenue to see the elaborately dressed bride doll. When the holidays were over, Mother repackaged the doll in its box, wrapped the box in a sheet remnant, and stowed it away in her large steamer trunk. There it remained, gaining liberty only on that rare occasion when my mother brought it out to display.

I was told that all of this happened that year, although I have little memory of it.

I do, however, have a clear picture of the following Easter Sunday. My mother had returned to her love affair with the sewing machine, and we were once again the stars of the Easter Parade. Those church sisters who were not seamstresses whispered that perhaps our outfits were a mite too gaudy and worldly for children of a saved and sanctified Christian. While Mother agonized over these comments, Father charged them to jealousy and did not give them another thought. Instead, he did as he had always done. He made himself available outside the church to receive the compliments offered by passersby.

His chest would swell with pride when he heard comments such as, "Are you sure Sister Sprague made William's suit. It looks tailor-made to me." "Look at that beautiful lace on Marvin's collar. I don't know how Sister Sprague does it."

Although Mother pretended to have no interest in the compliments, she would skillfully extract repeat renditions of them from my father. Such questions as, "Was it the pleats in Marvin's skirt that Sister Moore liked so much or was it the embroidered rosebuds on the puffed sleeves?" Or, "William, who was it that said, 'Why I thought little Bill was wearing that suit I saw in Hudson's window'?"

Father would smile and repeat, for the umpteenth time, the exact wording of the compliment.

To all outward appearances, this Easter seemed the same as any other Easter. The only indication to the contrary was reflected in the matter of the pink straw hat.

Being the baby of the family admittedly had its advantages, but they were often outweighed by the disadvantages. The matter of hand-me-down clothes was a case in point. Many of my friends claimed that they did not have new clothes until they were able to buy them for themselves. I was more fortunate. I also wore my sister's outgrown clothes, but they did not look like hand-me-downs. My mother would alter the look by crocheting a different collar, attaching a contrasting ruffle, or trimming the sleeves with a different binding.

Jewel had worn the pink straw hat several years before. My mother had planned for me to wear it the Easter before Jewel's death, but it didn't fit. She promised that I would wear it the following year. This year my mother had made a pink ribbon satin dress with puffed sleeves and a crocheted Peter Pan collar. When Uncle Smitty saw my dress, he said, "Gracie, it's a beautiful dress, but it definitely needs a pair of white Mary Jane shoes." My mother fussed and said I needed school shoes instead. My uncle agreed but bought the Mary Janes anyway. I could always depend on my uncle to do the right thing. Aunt Bessie bought me a pair of white cotton socks with embroidered white lace cuffs. With the pink hat, my Easter outfit was complete.

On Easter morning, Uncle Smitty came by early to see us in all our splendor. He smiled when he saw me and said, "Marvin, you're so pretty, even your walk has changed."

My mother immediately countered with, "Pretty is as pretty does!"

My uncle, as usual, insisted on having the last word. As he walked past my brother, he said, "May I at least call this young man handsome?"

My mother gave him a disgusted look and turned back to adjusting the pink hat. Finally, the hat was adjusted to her satisfaction, and she turned me around for my father's appraisal. As welcome as my uncle's compliments were, it was my father's approval that really mattered. He did not fail me. His praise reached lyrical heights. I was beautiful, gorgeous, a little princess, and a sight to behold. I did not bask in the flattery—I wallowed. Even in my delight, I waited in anticipation for Mother's usual conceit-destroying comments, but she remained curiously silent. As the silence lengthened, Father looked at her with a troubled expression on his face. He moved to sit beside her on the sofa and placed his arm around her. My mother buried her head in his shoulder as he softly murmured, "Gracie, Gracie, Gracie."

The sound of my mother's sobs filled the room. Father looked up and said, "William, you and Marvin go outside."

My brother led me outside to the back porch where we sat down on the top step of the stairwell. We sat in silence, waiting whatever fate had in store for us. Finally, my father came to the door and said, "You kids come in here and finish getting ready for Sunday school."

As I pushed past my father, he reached down and removed the pink hat from my head. Frowning at my mother, he said, "Gracie, I know I don't know much about style, but don't you think this hat is wrong for that dress. The dress is fussy, but the hat is tailored. Wouldn't a pink ribbon look better on Marvin?"

Although I did not understand what was going on between my mother and father, I could hear the relief in my mother's voice as she responded, "Maybe you're right. I knew something was bothering me about that hat. Marvin will still be able to wear it next year, and I can make her a suit to match."

Breathing a deep sigh, she took three pink satin ribbons from the ribbon box and tied one on each of my braids. Father spun my brother and me around for a quick examination, then declared us ready to face the world. Wearing appropriately serious expressions, we left for Sunday school. As we turned the corner of the walkway, I looked back to see my father and mother standing in the doorway with proud smiles on their faces. Whenever I think of them, this is the image I see.

The next year, I begged for an Easter outfit in my favorite color—blue. To go with it, Uncle Smitty bought the blue, lace-trimmed skimmer displayed in the front window of Ruben's Department Store. My mother accused me of begging for the hat, but my uncle stoutly defended me against her charge. When pressed, he said, "I swear on my mother's grave that Marvin never mentioned that hat."

He did fail to note, however, that I had pointed it out to him on several occasions.

My outfit received rave reviews from spectators at the Easter Parade. As for the pink straw hat, I never saw or heard of it again.

The Good Reverend

By the spring of 1935 our family had become an integral part of Herbert Street. It seems that nothing binds people together more than tragedy. In death my sister continued to work her wonders. It was her death more than anything else that brought the residents of Herbert Street together in a bond of trust and friendship.

It was a street with a split personality. Factory workers, domestic day workers, welfare families, and just plain hustlers, whose activities were better left unexplored, occupied buildings on our side of the street. Our side also could boast of a writer who lived in the small house on the alley. Five teachers, a doctor, several store clerks, a nurse, and numerous city, state, and federal employees occupied the north side of the street. Even one of Joe Louis's aunts lived in the large brick apartment building directly across the street from our flat.

Our family held a unique position in the neighborhood because of my father's job. Although we lived on the south side of Herbert Street, my father worked as a chef at a large downtown hotel. Prior to his marriage to my mother, he had served as a chef in several New Orleans restaurants and had also spent several years as a cook for a railroad work crew. The hotel he currently worked for did not dare list him on their work roster as a chef, so he was listed as a kitchen helper and paid chef wages under the table. He was much sought after for his knowledge of Creole cuisine. Only our family knew that earlier in life he had sung in the chorus of an opera company while serving as a chauffeur for the wife of a vice president of the U.S. Rubber Company while she was traveling abroad. It was his reward for keeping the lady out of harms way.

One Sunday morning, in the fall of 1935, a rumor raced through the neighborhood that the heavyweight champion of the Detroit Free Press Golden Gloves tournament, Joe Louis, would visit his aunt that afternoon. Sentinels were imme-

diately stationed at the corners of our block with strict orders to sound the alarm if anything remotely resembling a motorcade came into view. Promptly at 4:15 P.M., the motorcade arrived. Out stepped the Brown Bomber, who stopped, briefly, to wave at the cheering crowd, who answered with cries of "Ain't he good looking!"

It was said that some young ladies were so overcome with emotion that they almost fainted. Even though the champ was in full view for roughly ninety seconds, it was the general consensus of the crowd that the all-day vigil was time well spent. Amid the excitement, a sleek black Buick turned the corner and pulled into the driveway adjoining our house. Virtually unnoticed, the Reverend Alphons Saxon and family had arrived in our midst.

The Saxons created quite a stir in our community. Perhaps I should say the Reverend Saxon created quite a stir. His wife and daughter seemed pleasant enough, but their pale, faded appearance and soft, timid voices did not invite social overtures. They seemed to disappear into the background, becoming all but invisible. In contrast, Reverend Saxon appeared larger than life. Not only was he a large man but he also had a deep, robust voice and a correspondingly vibrant laugh. Parishioners marveled at his physical size and strength. In tones of awe and admiration, men were heard to say, "Did you see the size of his hands? Why, they're large enough to fit around my thigh!"

The Reverend reveled in the admiration and added to it by lifting one of the little Allen girls and sitting her, firmly, on one of his outstretched hands. This demonstration only added to the congregation's admiration for their tall, handsome spiritual leader. Mothers urged the Reverend to favor their young daughters by holding them securely aloft, supported only by the strong grip of his mammoth fingers. Only my father seemed unimpressed by the Reverend's physical prowess. He would stand aloof, eyes narrowed, and intently study the Reverend as he lifted his small charges high into the air. Once, I heard Uncle Smitty ask him, "Bill, what's wrong?" only to hear Father respond, "Next time he does that stunt, watch his reaction."

Try as I might, I saw nothing unusual, but my uncle later told my father that he thought it was an involuntary reaction and meant nothing. Despite my uncle's assurances, I often saw both men look at the Reverend with questioning eyes.

When word reached me that Beatrice, my ace boom buddy, my kindred spirit and best friend, was coming home, I soon lost interest in solving the mystery. Now I would be able to answer a question of far greater interest to me—why Beatrice had been sent to Chicago to stay with her sister. Last summer she had been suddenly uprooted and sent away, without so much as a goodbye. The grownups whispered among themselves—something about Beatrice and the little Kennedy girl—but even the most enterprising among us had been unable to discover what it was all about. Never mind. The important thing was that Beatrice was coming home!

Only one factor marred my joy at the return of my best friend. My loving and caring mother did not like Beatrice. While the knowledge of Mother's obvious distaste for Beatrice weighed heavily on my heart, Beatrice and I had sworn undying friendship, and friends we would remain. Father was aware of my mother's feelings and asked, "Why?"

"Why?" Mother answered. "You're suppose to be a man of the world, and you ask *why*?"

In a tightly controlled voice, Father wondered aloud, "Where's that Christian love you're always talking about? That child needs more love and understanding than we have to give!"

As I listened at the crack in their bedroom door, I heard nothing that would explain my mother's feelings. At seven years old, I was far too young to understand how the close friendship between her daughter and a super tomboy frightened my mother; however, a day would soon come that would forever change her negative opinion of Beatrice.

As the daylight hours grew short and chill winds began to blow through the cracks around the windows and doors, our thoughts turned to securing the Green House against the even stronger winds to come. Father put thick layers of putty around all the windows and doors. Mother made draft stoppers for the doors and windows out of scrap wool. Since our house was heated with coal-burning stoves, double loads of coal were ordered and stacked in the coal shed located behind the Saxon flat.

If there was one thing my brother and I agreed on, it was our distaste for making the cold, lonely trip to the coal shed. Our image of the shed changed with the seasons. In spring and summer, the shed served as safe haven to hide from our mother when she was seized by one of her seasonal cleaning frenzies. It served as a reading room and rehearsal hall for my brother, a place where he could safely read his science fiction magazines and practice the violin to his heart's content. I used it as a secret hideaway, a place where I could freely indulge my love of daydreaming without risking the ridicule of my friends. My brother had fitted the shed door with an additional inside lock. There, seated on top of the coal pile, I spent many happy hours mentally riding elephants in India, climbing mountains in Switzerland, and sailing down the Seine on a large flower-covered barge.

Winter and the shed was an entirely different matter. Ice made the path difficult to navigate; snow fell through the cracks in the roof, froze on the coal pile, and made it hard to shovel.

One cold, snowy afternoon, as I returned along the path loaded down with a heavy bucket of coal, I met Reverend Saxon, who smiled and said, "Hello."

I moved to skirt him but soon realized that he was still in front of me, blocking my path. As I looked up to see why he had not moved, he bent low and said, "What's a pretty little lady like you doing out alone so late in the afternoon?"

For a moment, only the words *pretty* and *lady* registered in my mind. The novelty of being described by such flattering words appealed to my childish vanity. The rosy glow generated by these words soon disappeared when I felt something wet on my cheek. As I touched it, I realized it had been left by the kiss the Reverend had placed there. Instinctively, I knew that something was very, very wrong.

As I struggled to break the Reverend's grip on my left arm, he tried to press some coins into my right hand. Simultaneously, he was mumbling, "Don't tell anyone, and I'll give you more money."

Panic gripped me, and I raised my foot and kicked him in the groin. Coins scattered everywhere as I broke free, raced back to the coal shed, and locked myself inside. Giant sobs racked my chest, and nervous tremors competed for control of my body. I heard Reverend Saxon at the shed door still mumbling, "Don't tell anyone! Don't tell anyone!"

After what seemed like an eternity, quiet descended. I slowly opened the door and tiptoed down the path. When I came to the spot where I had dropped the bucket, I gathered up the scattered coal and ran home.

I thought my mother would see that something was wrong, but all she said was, "What took you so long? It's getting late, and you still have to do your homework."

After supper I changed into my nightgown and huddled, still trembling, under the bedcovers. When daylight broke through the cracks in the window shade, I was still awake.

The next morning found me in front of Beatrice's house before she had finished breakfast. When Beatrice saw my face, she rushed to finish her oatmeal and join me. In silence we walked, side by side, to our secret meeting place. At the rear of Lothrop Library there was an iron security door surrounded by three large heating vents designed to release surplus steam from the heating system.

Even before we were seated on the step below the door, Beatrice asked, "What's wrong?"

I burst into tears as I told her the story. When I had finished, Beatrice sat in silence. "I don't know what to do! Tell me what to do," I said.

Suddenly, Beatrice came to life, saying, "I know what to do, come on."

She dragged me down the street past her house, up my back steps, and into the kitchen where my mother stood preparing lunch. Mother took one look at our faces and asked, "What's wrong?"

The tension was too much for me. I sat down on the floor and bawled like a baby. As always, it was Beatrice who saved the day. Calmly and clearly she told my mother the story, omitting not one detail.

When she had finished speaking, Mother sat for several minutes in silence. Finally, she rose from her chair, went to the cookie jar, and took out a handful of cookies for us, then grabbed her shawl from the hook by the back door, and after admonishing us to stay put, left the house. Immediately, we rushed outside to the section of the porch that overhung the entrance to the Saxon flat.

At first we could not hear what my mother said when Mrs. Saxon came to the door, though we risked life and limb in the attempt. As they continued talking, I heard her say, "Why would she lie? How would she know to lie?"

Finally, Mrs. Saxon pulled my mother inside, and the door closed behind them, smothering all sound.

Now that matters were out of our hands, we were suddenly very hungry. By the time my mother returned, we had consumed the cookies and started on some grapes we found in the icebox. After hanging up her shawl, she said, "Everything is taken care of, and we will not speak of this to anyone, especially your father."

Before the word *why* could form on my lips, Beatrice said, "No, Marvin. You must never tell your father, because he would kill Reverend Saxon, and they would put him in jail."

Mother nodded her head in fervent confirmation. The die was cast. Wild horses could not drag the secret from me.

As Beatrice stood up to leave, my mother embraced her and placed a thank-you kiss on her cheek. An expression of complete joy flashed across Beatrice's face.

When Mother assured us that all would be well, we did not expect such dramatic results. The next morning an excited assistant pastor awakened us. The Reverend and his family had just left his house. It seemed an emergency had developed in the Reverend's family, and he had to rush to Alabama at once. The assistant pastor was puzzled, however, because the Saxon car was loaded with luggage, and an attached trailer held most of their furniture. When asked when he would return, the Reverend had promised to stay in touch and to relay his future plans as soon as they were firm.

The Good Reverend was never seen again.

The congregation of the Church of the True Believers mourned his loss as if mourning the death of a favorite son. The assistant pastor tried valiantly to fill his shoes but was considered a dismal failure by all.

Despite the general consensus that the assistant pastor was inadequate, the appointment of the Reverend Jacqueline Elder divided both friends and families. Only my mother was heard to say, "There are worse things on this earth then having a woman minister."

Christmas came, and with it a grudging acceptance of Reverend Elder. By the following spring, she was proudly referred to as "our pastor" by one and all. As for my mother and me, we never spoke of the Good Reverend Saxon again.

MY FATHER VS. THE CHURCH
OF THE TRUE BELIEVERS

On the question of whether my father was a saint or a sinner, opinions were split. The majority of people in our neighborhood thought him a man of honor, wisdom, and integrity—someone you would be proud to call a friend. To the Church of the True Believers, he symbolized all that the Church stood against. Both opinions had some validity.

As my mother was a devout member of the Church of the True Believers, the church's opinion of my father could have created a problem for my parents. Rest assured, however, that the church's negative viewpoint had no impact on my mother's complete adoration of my father. Father returned this adoration in full measure, pressed down and overflowing. Although the elders of the church often enjoined the members of the congregation to pray for "poor Sister Sprague," they were careful to do so only on nights when Mother was absent from her pew.

Where did it all begin? Perhaps with my father's obvious distaste for the rigid doctrine taught by the Church. He would mutter under his breath, "What makes them think they have a monopoly on knowing the will of God."

My father believed that this earth was created to give mankind pleasure, not to constrain and punish him for imaginary sins. He often said, "There's nothing under the sun that's inherently evil; good or evil depends on a person's intent."

In the eyes of my mother's church, to think such thoughts was bad enough, but to speak them aloud was blasphemy.

If memory serves me right, the first major altercation between Father and the church was known as the Chicken Legs Fracas. It was generated by a practice long engaged in by the spiritual mothers of the church. It was their custom to favor one of the church sisters with a Sunday visit, usually around dinnertime. Since Father was a chef, our house was favored more than most. Even I could sense my father's growing anger as Sunday after Sunday we shared our dinner hour with first one then another of the church mothers. The Sunday that Mother Blevins reached across the table and deftly swept both chicken legs onto her plate was the Sunday my father totally lost control. In a voice like thunder, he roared, "Madam! The chicken legs are reserved for my children. You are welcome to any other pieces of chicken, but the legs are for my children!"

A shocked hush fell over the room. Finally, Mother Blevins regained her composure, and with an angry "I'll pray for you Sister Sprague," she swept across the room, down the stairs, and out the front gate. Mother, holding back tears, jumped up from the table and ran into the kitchen, slamming the door behind her.

Father put on his hat and said, "Tell your mother I'll be back shortly," then left the house.

By the time he returned, everything appeared to be back to normal. If there was any later discussion of the incident, it took place well out of our earshot.

The next Sunday, Mother silenced all comers by reminding them that Mr. Sprague worked hard to put food on his table, and the chicken legs were for his children. Since many of the loudest agitators often set their dinner tables with leftovers supplied by my father, the subject was soon dropped.

In retrospect, this incident might well have been the bellwether of what we now call the children's rights movement. I do know that every neighborhood child old enough to comprehend the meaning of the words *equality* and *justice* hailed my father as a hero. Children, whose dinners on the Sundays that a church mother visited consisted only of gravy, mashed potatoes, and green peas, now found at least a chicken wing nestled beside the biscuits on their plates.

Time passed, and an uneasy truce settled over the battlefield. It was the Miss Lillian and Mr. Levi dilemma that brought the animosity between the church and my father to a boiling point.

The neighborhood first knew Miss Lillian as Mrs. Joe Thompson. She lived, along with her husband and five children, in the little house on the alley. The family eked out a living from Mr. Thompson's illegal numbers business and Mrs. Thompson's home-based laundry service. They were that family present in every community who serves as the there-but-for-the-grace-of-God-go-I example.

When Joe Thompson deserted his family, after making sure to tell the local gossips that his Mrs. was really not his Mrs., the family slipped even farther down the social totem pole. Overnight, Mrs. Thompson became Miss Lillian.

While several husbands in the neighborhood made pests of themselves trying to start affairs with Miss Lillian, it was the neighborhood wives who effectively nailed her to the cross. Their children were no longer allowed to play with the Thompson children. Several ladies gave Miss Lillian discarded clothing—clothing fit only to be cut into dust cloths. Mrs. Roe gave her several bags of dried milk that proved, upon opening, to be alive with worms. Unfortunately, Miss Lillian also carried the burden of being a beautiful woman.

Although Mother did not join the parade of ladies conspicuous in their attempts to do their Christian duty, Father more than compensated for my mother's apparent oversight by providing large pans of leftovers from the hotel kitchen. When he told the head chef about the family's plight, the chef began leaving packages of food buried in the outside garbage containers for Father to take to the family.

"Well," Mother said, "at least they won't starve to death."

Still, I wondered why my mother wasn't personally involved in helping the Thompson family. The answer to that question was not long in coming.

In early March, Mother made her annual trek to the children's department of Hudson's Department Store. Her purpose was not to purchase but to study the new Easter frocks with an eye for copying one as my Easter outfit. Mother was an expert seamstress and was often hired by affluent society types to copy designer frocks for their wardrobes. She had a photographic memory and could study a dress for a few minutes, then return home and replicate it perfectly, down to the last detail. After one of the Hudson buyers caught her making a sketch of a particularly tricky sleeve on a Chanel design, she was barred from Hudson's designer shops. My mother simply purchased used copies of *Vogue* and *Harpers Bazaar* fashion magazines and continued her work. The trips she made to the designer shops were business trips, but the trips she made to the children's department were labors of love.

Once Mother decided on the style of my dress, she made a pattern out of brown paper. This pattern was carefully arranged and rearranged to assure the most economical use of material. Then, the sewing began. The whir of the sewing machine could be heard halfway down the block. Meals were erratic, at best, but no one complained because Easter Sunday was close at hand. Soon my new Easter outfit hung on the back of my bedroom door, sharing space with my brother's new blue jacket and sharply creased, black wool slacks.

With our outfits finished, I began to wonder why Mother continued to pound on the old Singer sewing machine. As I watched her work, I began to understand the "why" of her efforts. Mother was fashioning Easter outfits for the Thompson children. For the girls, blue jumpers and white blouses, and for the boys, blue plaid shirts and dark blue knickers.

On Easter Sunday, the Thompson children, scrubbed and polished within an inch of their lives, sat with our family in front row seats at the Church of the True Believers. The irony of the situation was not lost on some of the church members, because throughout the Thompson's troubles, the church had remained curiously silent. Never had I felt prouder of my mother than I did that day.

As the months passed, interest in Miss Lillian's plight waned. Only a few people continued to secretly supply the family with food and the occasional dollar. It was an unexpected incident that revived local interest, unfortunately, in a negative way.

One evening in early October, passersby noticed the tantalizing odor of fried fish coming from Miss Lillian's house. To understand the significance of this incident, you must understand the role fish played as a status symbol in our society. Fresh fish was an expensive commodity not usually found on our dinner tables. On the rare occasion that someone in the neighborhood went fishing and returned with a large catch, the fish kettles were fired up, and a neighborhood fish fry ensued. My father would bring out our Victrola and some dance records, and the fish fry would become a fish festival. Of course my father's involvement in this Sodom-and-Gomorra exercise did nothing to enhance his standing with the church.

The first question asked was, "How could Miss Lillian afford to buy fish?"

The answer came from the mouth of the little Robinson girl, who said, "Oh, Mr. Levi gave Miss Lillian the fish."

Under interrogation by the ladies, Loretta described how that afternoon Mr. Levi had taken Miss Lillian into the back of the fish market, wrapped two fish in newspaper, and handed the package to her. As she turned to leave, he had gently kissed her on the cheek.

This information left the good ladies gasping for words. My mother described it as a sight well worth any price of admission.

Only my father seemed to feel it was much ado about nothing. "After all," he said, "they are both unmarried and over twenty-one."

I think the real problem was that Miss Lillian was a Negro and Mr. Levi was a Jew. In the end, even Father agreed the situation might further tarnish Miss Lillian's reputation. It was a problem that required resolution. As if to prove the point, the following Sunday the congregation of the Church of the True Believers voted to expel Miss Lillian from membership in the church. Only my mother, Aunt Bessie, and Reverend Elder voted in the negative.

During the next few days, both Miss Lillian's house and the fish market were under constant surveillance. It was inevitable that Father's meeting with Mr. Levi was observed. Although the entire neighborhood was desperate to know the content of the conversation, none dared approach Father to broach the subject. When Father came home, he whispered something into my mother's ear. Mother laughed and said, "I can't wait to see their faces when they learn what's going on."

All in all, Father seemed quite pleased with himself.

Several weeks later, Mr. Levi pulled up to Miss Lillian's house in a brand-new red Chevrolet convertible. He went inside, and in a few minutes escorted Miss Lillian and the children out to the car. Was that really Miss Lillian? She wore a pink silk dress with a sweetheart neckline. Two strands of white pearls graced her slender neck, and teardrop earrings shimmered on her earlobes. The children were dressed in the Easter outfits my mother had made for them. Wearing a wide smile, Mr. Levi tipped his hat to the neighborhood ladies and then drove away.

When they returned, a moving van was waiting in front of the little house on the alley. It took less than an hour for the little house to surrender its contents to the van. The red convertible, followed by the tightly packed van, exited the driveway, rounded the corner, and passed from view. A haze seemed to settle over the neighborhood as the crowd slowly dispersed to their homes.

In anticipation of my father's return from work, the crowd began to assemble on our front porch at about six o'clock that evening. After all, whatever pledge of secrecy my father had made to Mr. Levi was no longer valid. The plan had been executed, and everything was now fair game. Surely he was now free to tell them the whole story. The crowd's curiosity was at fever pitch when the hotel dishwasher brought my mother a message. Father would be very late as an unexpected government delegation had checked into the hotel and preparations were underway for a formal reception to be held the next day. Reluctantly, the crowd departed, vowing to return the next day.

Early the next morning the crowd began to reassemble. At seven o'clock my mother went to the door to advise the group that my father was just having his breakfast but would be out soon. That day I learned the true meaning of power. As Father leisurely finished his breakfast, the crowd sat, immobile, in anticipation of the revelations to come.

Finally, he came out, sat down, and prepared to reveal the secret details of the Lillian-Levi affair.

As Father started to speak, someone realized that Mrs. Smedley, the neighborhood matriarch, was not present. Two teenagers were immediately dispensed to bring her to the meeting. There was much clearing of throats and tapping of toes until the boys came into view almost carrying Mrs. Smedley. Once Mrs. Smedley was safely in her seat of honor beside my father, he was free to begin.

Father had started his conversation with Mr. Levi by reminding him of their long friendship. He also told him that he had long been aware of his feelings for Miss Lillian. When Mr. Levi asked, "How did you know?" my father replied, "By the way you look at her."

Mr. Levi had hung his head and mumbled, "I wouldn't hurt Miss Lillian for anything in the world."

My father agreed that this might be true but said that a clandestine affair did little to help her. After this exchange, they both stood, silently considering the situation.

Suddenly, my father said, "If you love her, and she loves you, why don't you two just get married?"

My father later told my mother that he actually saw the light go on in Levi's head.

"Do you think she would marry me?" Mr. Levi had asked.

"Well," answered my father, "you'll never know if you never ask."

Having planted the seeds of resolution, my father left it to Mr. Levi to think it through.

Once the decision was made, roadblocks fell one by one. Mr. Levi's older brothers and sisters lived in Flint, Michigan. They had long urged their younger brother to move to Flint and open a fish market. One brother had even researched the area and found that there was not a fish market within a thirty-mile radius.

When Mr. Levi's relatives met Miss Lillian, they fell head over heels in love with her. Mr. Levi's oldest sister owned a small house on the east side of Flint in an area that bordered a Negro section. It stood empty and would be an excellent first home for the happy couple. So the die was cast, and just like in the movies, the Levi family rode off into the sunset.

After Father finished speaking, the crowd sat for a while, basking in the magic glow of that rare happy ending. Of course they knew that an interracial marriage presented unique problems of its own, but they also knew happiness, even temporary happiness, was well worth the effort.

Reluctantly, they began to move out for the workday that lay ahead—the fortunate few to paying jobs, the unfortunate many to job assignments with the Works

Projects Administration, a program designed to compensate the government for welfare funds received. Momentarily, they had been lifted above their humdrum, everyday lives, and they were grateful.

In the months that followed, Father's war with the church drifted into an unofficial cease-fire, and Mother continued to attend the Church of the True Believers. In time, however, I noticed that she listened to the minister less but read her Bible more. She appeared altogether the better for it.

TAKE FROM NO BIRD HER SONG

As much as my father loved his children, my mother held center stage in his life. She was a beautiful woman by any standard but worked hard to downplay her attractiveness. From her plain black nurses' oxfords, heavy lisle stockings, zipper-front house dresses to the pulled-back bun that confined her thick shoulder-length hair, she fought, valiantly, to project an image of plainness. Despite her best efforts, she failed miserably.

On the other hand, Father was a bit of a dandy. He loved tailor-made clothes, Italian shoes, and Borsalonia hats. Until my father married my mother, he had never bought a suit off a store rack in his adult life. Even his work pants carried a razor-sharp crease.

My parents were a perfect example of the maxim that opposites attract. He was the lead actor, but she set the stage for his performance.

My mother knew everything. I would rush home from school to dazzle her with some new information I had learned that day only to have her further define and expand on the subject. I later learned that my mother had been exposed to books all of her life. Her father had a love of books that bordered on addiction. He passed this sweet addiction on to her.

One of Mother's most devoted friends was Miss Pleasant. We children made fun of her name, but we all knew that it fit. She was a very pleasant person. Miss Pleasant would always laugh at our knock-knock jokes no matter how stupid they were. Many members of the Church of the True Believers called her simple minded, but my mother always said, "She's just closer to God than the rest of us."

Miss Pleasant would come to our house shortly after lunch on weekdays and keep my mother company while she prepared the evening meal. They held little conversation but seemed to be perfectly comfortable just being in each other's company. Several of my friends would come and sit on the steps leading from the kitchen to the backyard waiting for Miss Pleasant to speak the words. Miss Pleasant had a phrase she used over and over again that really cracked us up. She had difficulty pronouncing the word *imagine* and would always pronounce it *remagine*. Each time she would repeat the phrase "Well, can you remagine," we would giggle and choke back laughter. After Miss Pleasant left, Mother would admonish us to "Take from no bird her song. After all, it's the spirit behind the words that matters, not the words themselves."

We always nodded our heads yes, although we didn't understand a word she said. Later that summer, my mother had an opportunity to demonstrate the meaning of those words.

Each year, Mother entered the numerous food contests held by church and school fairs in the area and took the top prize. Some of the fairs experienced such a large decrease in entries that they asked my mother to enter her famous peach preserves only every other year. In alternate years she would enter her equally famous cha-cha relish and take the top prize in the pickle and relish category.

Every year I would ask her, "Why don't you enter the state fair contest?" She would smile, pat my head, and say, "That would be a complete waste of time."

I didn't know that she had entered her peach preserves and cha-cha relish one year and won both top prizes. When she came forward to receive her ribbons, the judges did not believe that she was the Grace Sprague listed on the entry forms. Only after the clerk who had registered her entries stepped forward and validated her identity did they release her first-place ribbons. For the next three years my mother submitted entries but never received so much as an honorable mention.

Canning season marked the beginning of a two-week period of frenzied activity. The kitchen windows were covered with steam from early morning until late night. Bushel baskets of fruits and vegetables were everywhere. Every hand was pressed into service to peel fruit, slice cucumbers, chop onions, tomatoes, and green peppers, wash Mason jars, and stir the pots of jams and jellies that covered every stove burner.

My friends and I kept a close watch on the sinfully tasty array of jams, jellies, mincemeats, and apple butters. We hung around the back door after school in case my mother needed taste testers. We would get to scrape the empty pots while my father and his friends were offered small saucers of jelly or jam along with a communal platter of fresh, hot biscuits.

When the frenzy finally subsided, the table, counters, and any other surface capable of sustaining weight were covered with processed Mason jars. Jars of soup mix, apple butter, green beans, mixed greens, strawberry jelly, and peach preserves were stacked in the pantry as silent warriors to guard against the shortage of fresh food so common during a long Michigan winter.

My mother considered the feeding of everyone who came into our home as both a pleasure and a responsibility. The fact that she enjoyed the accolades that invariably followed was, supposedly, of minor concern. Yet when Father teased her about the obvious pride she took in her culinary skills, she would laugh and say, "Take from no bird her song."

Although I would ask her repeatedly, "What does that mean, Mama?" she was never able to explain in a way I could understand.

In early September a Mrs. Washington moved into the neighborhood. A widow with three children, she lived on welfare. Since most families in the neighborhood had more than a passing acquaintance with the welfare system, this fact was barely noticed. What did generate avid discussion was Mrs. Washington's obvious lack of any housekeeping or culinary skills.

Mrs. Washington's children were always dirty and often barefoot. Some ladies counted the number of consecutive days they wore the same clothes—one week the count reached five days. The Washington children were always begging food. They soon learned that if they came and stood in our kitchen door, they would be fed. Father grumbled about the extra loaves of bread Mother baked but stilled his tongue after she sent a piercing glance his way.

Against this background, it really took everyone by surprise when Mrs. Washington bragged, "I make the best cha-cha relish in the world."

Those who tasted it reported back to my mother, saying, "It's pretty good cha-cha, but it can't hold a candle to yours."

As the canning season rolled along, Father's closest friends would come, one by one, to beg a small jar of preserves or jelly as an early Christmas present.

As usual, the entries for the church's October fair were prepared last. This allowed my mother to concentrate solely on the preparation of whatever items she had decided to enter. This year it would be cha-cha relish and soup mix.

One afternoon, when I ran in from school and announced that Mrs. Washington was entering cha-cha relish at the church fair, all activity ceased.

When conversation resumed, Aunt Bessie said, "Gracie, maybe you could enter some pickled beets instead."

Mother answered, "Yes, but would it satisfy her to win that way?"

Aunt Bessie shrugged her shoulders and said, "Gracie, you have two choices. Either enter your cha-cha or enter something else."

As my aunt spoke, my mother reached for the container of special spices she used to season the cha-cha, moved to the large pot of relish simmering on the stove, and added two heaping spoonfuls of the mix to the contents.

Aunt Bessie exclaimed, "I thought we agreed the flavor was just right! Why, you'll ruin the relish!"

Mother did not answer but continued to stir the pot. The oddest expression crossed my aunt's face, and she dropped her head. Finally, she said, "All right, Miss Gracie!" as she continued to sterilize the Mason jars to be used for the relish.

When Father came home, he fussed about the clutter that littered the kitchen. Even while he fussed, he smiled as he looked around at the stacks of canned food that covered every available surface. He tore a chunk off a loaf of bread sitting in a pan on the kitchen table and dipped it into the pot of relish simmering on the stove. As he threw his head back and tossed the relish-soaked bread into his mouth, Aunt Bessie casually mentioned, "Mrs. Washington is entering cha-cha relish in the pickle and relish category of the church fair competition and stands a good chance of winning."

As Father chewed on the bread, he frowned. Hesitatingly, he said to my mother, "This batch is not quite up to your usual standards. Do you want me to chop some more vegetable so you can make another batch?"

Mother refused, saying, "It really isn't that important, and anyway there's always next year."

Father started to insist, but Aunt Bessie slyly repeated her statement. "Mrs. Washington is entering her cha-cha relish in the pickle and relish category."

Suddenly, Father laughed and said, "Practicing what you preach, Gracie?" He grabbed her around the waist and danced her around the kitchen, while we children squealed with delight.

The following Saturday, Mrs. Washington won the blue ribbon for her cha-cha relish in the pickle and relish category at the church fair.

THE BOYS OF SUMMER

They came in April, the boys of summer. Resplendent in pastel-colored gabardine suits, wearing faded winter tans, they were the first wave of a two-part pilgrimage that took place yearly, as my father would say, "come hell or high water." They were the true harbingers of spring.

The first wave drove their brightly colored convertibles with the tops up. The second wave, which usually arrived late in May, drove with the tops down, flaunting the butter-soft tan, brown, or black leather upholstery tailor-made for their customized cars. Every time Father saw them, his facial expression would harden into that of an angry old man. He said that although they called themselves survey takers, they were actually con men who did their job well. After the first year, they did not survey our house.

When my father first opened the door to them, he took their measure in full. They were in the neighborhood to take a survey, or so they said, and could he spare a few minutes to answer some questions for a young man working his way through college? Father did not answer but kept his eyes trained on the bright pink Chevrolet convertible visible through the open door.

The questions asked seemed strange to me, but Father appeared to understand them completely. What are your favorite radio programs? Name as many as you can think of.

He smiled and replied, "Kraft Music Hall, Hallmark Hall of Fame, Texaco Theater, the six o'clock news, and, oh yes, Saturday afternoon broadcasts from the Metropolitan Opera."

Suddenly, the atmosphere changed. The young men slammed their folders shut, snapped out "thank you," and rushed downstairs to the Davis apartment. I thought I heard the one with dark hair mumble, "Smart ass nigger," as he trailed the others down the steps. My father just laughed and shut the door. Winking at Mother, he said, "They'll find what they're looking for down there."

All that day they flitted from door to door, asking questions, teasing the ladies of the house, and promising to return the next month to take anyone who wanted to go for a ride in their glistening convertibles. After they left, there was much laughing and comparing of notes between the ladies of the neighborhood. Why, there hadn't been this much excitement since Joe Louis paid his aunt a surprise visit.

It wasn't until church services on Sunday that Mother learned what all the excitement was about. It seemed that the young men had taken much more than a survey. They had also taken orders for sweaters—soft angora sweaters—in rainbow colors of pink, baby blue, canary yellow, lime green, vibrant red, chalk white, and ebony black. For the more adventurous, there were shades of fuchsia, turquoise, wine, and magenta. The mind boggled at the range of styles and colors. To think they were all available for only fifty cents down and twenty-five cents a week. Some of the ladies said they felt a little guilty taking advantage of such nice young men. When Father heard this, he snorted and said, "Taking advantage! Fifty cents down and twenty-five cents a week for the rest of their lives."

He could have saved his breath. For the first time in memory, the neighborhood neither sought nor accepted my father's counsel. The ladies' only concern was for the safe arrival of the sweaters they had ordered. Mother, always loath to admit that she did not understand something, finally broke down and asked Father the question that had been churning around in her head. "William, what does a survey have to do with selling sweaters?"

Father answered, "That's just their way of determining if the people in the neighborhood are dumb enough to be taken in by their scam. If they listen to silly programs, they are probably silly people. That's why my answers to their questions angered them so. They knew I understood the name of the game they were playing."

Mother nodded her head and then said, "Now why didn't I think of that? You always said they were thinking while we were sleeping."

True to their word, the young men were back in less than a month, laden with boxes of ladies' sweaters in assorted colors. A holiday atmosphere invaded the neighborhood. The ladies followed the salesmen from house to house as they delivered orders. A spirit of competition soon set in. Those who had ordered only one or two sweaters asked for more as they witnessed five and six sweaters being delivered to their neighbors. The salesmen had wisely brought along extra sweaters and were able to fill their requests.

When the smoke cleared, many ladies had overextended themselves but were too proud to admit it. They would pull a salesman to the side and ask for additional credit, promising to pay the fifty-cent deposit the following week as well as double the twenty-five-cent weekly fee. The salesman graciously accepted their offer but warned that, since he would be making up the deposits out of his own pocket, he would have to charge interest. The ladies agreed to his terms—after all, it was only interest on fifty cents. As a bonus, the salesmen gave each customer a set of angora socks. It was late afternoon before the salesmen finished their deliveries and drove off, horns blowing. Amid the excitement, Father sat on our porch reading the evening newspaper.

The next Sunday, and for several Sundays to follow, the Church of the True Believers resembled a flower garden far more than the home of a saved and sanctified congregation. The seats of the sanctuary were filled with ladies of every age and description decked out in a rainbow of brightly colored angora sweaters. Although Reverend Elder admonished the congregation not to be taken in by the "garish things of this world," the number of members wearing sweaters increased week by week.

Gradually, the sweater craze reached a climax, and the number of ladies wearing them slipped significantly, then dropped to almost zero. Only a few diehards among the young folk persisted in wearing them long after they had become the worse for wear. Mrs. Robinson, who had purchased four, confessed to my mother, "No matter how carefully I wash them, they just fall apart."

Suddenly, the door was opened. One by one, purchasers of sweaters began to complain about their quality. If they did not fall apart, they faded or lost their shape. In only a few short weeks, most were unwearable. The nadir of discontent came when several ladies began to use their sweaters as dust clothes—it was said they made wonderful dust catchers.

While the sweaters gradually disappeared, the salesmen did not. Every Saturday, regular as clockwork, they would arrive to collect their weekly fees and update the customers' payment booklets. My father was right. It seemed that the ladies would be paying for those sweaters for the rest of their lives. Even the customers who made payments on a regular basis were never completely paid up. Those who missed several payments fell hopelessly behind. Customers who balked at making further payments, citing the shoddiness of the merchandise, were threatened with legal action. The threat alone was enough to whip them back in line. All during the turmoil, Father sat on our porch reading the evening newspaper.

The Fourth of July came and went, and still the boys of summer made their collections every Saturday. The payment booklets were so haphazardly annotated that even the most vigilant customers soon gave up in despair and accepted whatever balance they were given. It was not until just before Christmas that the last balance due was paid off. When my mother relayed the news to my father, he signed and said, "I hope they've finally learned their lesson."

During the week between Christmas and New Year, my father worked many overtime hours helping out at the Detroit Sheraton Hotel. In the year 1939, the poor were getting poorer, but the rich were getting richer. The downtown hotels were booked solid for dinners, banquets, and luncheons. Theaters and clubs offered the very best acts in the entertainment world. Downtown Detroit was awash with bright lights, glittering decorations, and beautiful people. The crowds in front of the Hudson's Department Store Christmas displays were at least three rows deep. There was something for everyone. When Uncle Smitty said, "Bill, you need to slow down, it's a wonder you don't fall asleep on the bus ride home and miss your stop," my father replied, "I'll rest later, I have to take advantage of the overtime while it's available."

It was on such a night that my father, while leaning against the front window of Sam's Cut Rate Department Store, glanced up and saw an enormous display of ladies' angora sweaters. The display lights had been left on, and the sweaters sparkled like jewels in the tinted lights. Across the top of the display was a banner pronouncing SALE! SALE! SALE! YOUR CHOICE, ONLY $1.69 EA OR 2 FOR $3.00.

Father went door to door on Herbert Street telling everyone about the angora sweaters available at Sam's Cut Rate Department Store. He had talked with a salesman and discovered they could be put in layaway with no additional charge. Since he passed the store every day on his way to and from work, he offered to act as a go-between—buying or making payments on sweaters for anyone who might be interested. He explained that this way the ladies could purchase sweaters practically pain free. Of the thirty, or more, families who lived on Herbert Street, only five accepted his offer. Although he had hoped for more takers, Father was not discouraged. Mother said, "At least it's a step in the right direction. When they see the superior quality of these sweaters, more people will want them."

Mother was right. More people did order the sweaters. While not the most expensive sweaters in the world, their quality far exceeded that of the sweaters sold by the boys of summer. Long after the holiday season was over, the sweaters graced many members of my mother's church.

Gradually, the days warmed as the calendar moved toward spring and the Easter renewal. Although winter was not quite over, the occasional unseasonably warm day held promise for the future. Front doors were left slightly ajar, and windows were raised in an attempt to air out the houses and chase away the winter doldrums. Clotheslines were put up, and sheets were seen flapping in the wind—often frozen solid. No matter, we had survived another winter, and that was a miracle in itself.

They came in April. The boys of summer. They went from house to house renewing old acquaintances while apologizing for the misunderstandings of the previous year. They spoke of how disappointed they had been with the quality of the merchandise provided by their supplier. They felt cheated, and they knew their customers must have felt cheated too. In fact, they felt so badly about the situation that this year they would reduce the down payment per sweater to twenty-five cents, with weekly payments of only twenty cents.

Their former customers were deeply moved. Mrs. Robinson said, "Gracie, I really feel sorry for them. You know the way that supplier took advantage of them is a sin and a shame. I told them not to worry. That no good comes out of evil!"

The salesmen took orders at a rapid rate. Most of those who had ordered the previous year reordered, along with several recent arrivals in the neighborhood. Mother exclaimed in amazement, "William, I wouldn't be surprised if they got twice as many orders as they did last year." Father did not respond. He seemed not to hear her.

All day they flitted from door to door, asking questions, teasing the lady of the house, and promising to return the next month to take anyone who wanted to go for a ride in their glistening new convertibles. After they left, there was much laughing and comparing of notes between the ladies of the neighborhood. Amid the excitement, Father sat unnoticed on our front porch reading the evening newspaper.

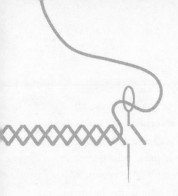

To Thine Own Self Be True

If the Church of the True Believers was my mother's sanctuary, then Lothrop Library was mine. I can remember my first visit to the public library as if it were yesterday. Our third grade teacher had promised the class a fieldtrip as a treat. The destination was to be a surprise. Our fertile nine-year-old minds bent to the task of solving the puzzle with gusto. Some thought it would be a trip to Belle Isle, while others opted for a visit to the Stroh's Ice Cream Factory. Those with more imaginative minds even suggested the possibility of a trip to a foreign country—Canada. In the end, we were left to wait on time to be proven right or wrong.

On the morning of the trip, we marched out the front door of Sill School and into a waiting bus. With many waves and shouts of goodbye, we set out for a destination yet unknown. The bus proceeded down Thirtieth Street, stopped to turn right onto Warren Avenue, then moved east on Warren until it reached West Grand Boulevard where a red light brought it to an abrupt stop. From the back of the bus, we could hear Mary Elizabeth Smith and Marie Cooper crowing, "I told you so! I told you so!"

They had put their faith in the treat being a trip to Stroh's. Although Beatrice and I hated to admit it, it did seem that we would head down Warren to Woodward Avenue and then south to the ice cream factory. The light turned green, and the driver turned right onto West Grand Boulevard and pulled up in front of Lothrop Library.

The odds of thirty-one nine-year-olds all losing their voice at the same time are probably, in the words of my mother's friend Miss Pleasant, a hundred, million, trillion to one. But as the bus driver killed the engine and opened the front door, those odds dropped, considerably. Miss Benson seemed puzzled by the silence but was reassured when the conversation level again rose to epic proportions. If she had been listening closely, she would have noticed a decided difference in the nature of the comments. From the back of the bus came, "I thought she said it would be a treat!" Another voice, which echoed the sentiments of many, said, "I knew it was too good to be true!" It was Beatrice who topped all other comments when she said, "Why, we could have walked up here."

It was a very downcast group that filed into the library with one exception. From the moment I entered the anteroom and smelled the odor of books grown worn and musty from use at the hands of people who loved them, I knew I was finally home.

My love affair with Lothrop Library was slow in developing but not by choice. At nine years old, my mother did not allow me to walk to the library by myself. Until the age of ten, my access to the Library was controlled by the most unlikely of dictators, my brother. Since he was very fond of his science fiction magazines, he had little need to visit the library for additional reading material. I was allowed to withdraw only two books per visit, but I read at the rate of a book a day. On average, my brother visited the library two days a week, which left me without reading material at least three days of the week.

Finally, the head librarian took mercy on me. One day she asked me to tell her about one of the books I was returning. She listened closely to my version of the story, then said, "Marvin, you're a fast reader. I'm going to make an exception in your case. You may withdraw four books per visit."

I sighed with relief, because I knew I had met a kindred spirit.

At first, I thought I stood alone in my affection for the library. Although I sometimes met classmates at the library, they always seemed to be in a hurry, rushing to leave as soon as they saw me come in. I later learned that there were a great many more closet readers then I imagined. If you loved to read, you were considered an egghead, and there was absolutely nothing worse than to be considered an egghead. My brother, however, was a prime example of the proverbial exception that proves the rule. He was a natural born egghead and seemed proud of it. It was a different situation for me. Since I knew the severity of this fault, and the constant teasing it could generate, I became quite adept at cloaking my affliction. No one bothered to tease my brother. There isn't much satisfaction in teasing a person who doesn't react.

The rules that determined whether you were an egghead were complex at best. Reading books weighed heavily against you, while attending the weekly story hour at Lothrop Library was considered perfectly all right. Each Tuesday afternoon, at 4:30 P.M., the conference room at the library was filled to overflowing with members of the Lothrop Library Story Hour Club. There, for one hour, a librarian would read to us from the book of the week. There were few boys in attendance, and those who were claimed to be there only to walk their younger brothers and sisters home. It was the boys, however, who complained most bitterly when the hour ended just as the story was heating up. The librarian would smile and remind them that they could always check the book out and finish reading the story at home. There was never a response to this statement, but if you checked the shelf the next day, that book would be missing.

Year after year, season after season, my love affair with the library continued. Occasionally, some exciting neighborhood event would slow the pace of my visits, but always the memory of those hundreds and hundreds of books would draw me back. Father had once told me that all knowledge was contained, somewhere, between the pages of a book. I was determined to prove or disprove this theory for myself. I read on and on. The *Five Little Peppers and How They Grew*, *Little Women*, the Bro Rabbit stories, the Nancy Drew stories, *Wind in the Willows*, these were just a few titles on my list.

One day, shortly before my twelfth birthday, I approached the checkout desk in despair. I had found only one book on the children's side that I had not read. The clerk looked at my face, then called the head librarian over. Hesitantly, she said, "Mrs. McMillan, for about two months Marvin's been having a problem finding books to take out. I believe she's read out the children's side of the library. Is there anything that can be done?"

Mrs. McMillan thought for a moment, then said, "It's never been tried before, but we could issue her a restricted adult card. We would have to closely monitor the books she selects, but it would solve the problem."

Miracle of miracles, I had gained unexpected entry into that most holy of places, the adult side of the public library. Before that day, I had only been able to look across the shelves that separated the children's side from the adult side and wonder what strange, forbidden fruit lay just across the way. Now I was free to investigate this Garden of Eden of the written word for myself.

The time I spent at the library increased significantly. I would scour the shelves for hours, selecting books, reading excerpts, always on the alert for books that would increase my knowledge of a certain subject—which I knew little about—the nature of love relationships between men and women. I knew that the books that touched on this subject would be off-limits to withdraw, but I soon realized that, while I was in the library, I could read anything I wanted to. I now had two selection criteria, one for books I planned to withdraw, and another for those I planned to read on the library premises.

Like all good plans, this one was open to human error. One afternoon I noticed there was a new clerk on the checkout desk. The day before, I had picked up a book entitled *The Captain Takes a Wife* and briefly scanned its pages. I was amazed to come across a passage that described a sexual liaison between two of the characters in rather explicit detail. Looking back, I am sure the description was as tame as dirt, but for its day and time, it was most daring. I knew this not from an intellectual level but from my memory of the events that followed its discovery.

Seeing the new clerk alone at her station, I quickly approached the desk, sandwiching *The Captain Takes a Wife* between two other novels. Imagine my surprise when the clerk stepped to the office door and asked, "Mrs. McMillan, is Marvin Sprague still allowed to check out books from the adult side?"

Mrs. McMillan looked up and said, "Yes, Marvin has a restricted adult card."

I was still shaking as I turned the corner of Herbert Street and headed for home.

The next day, I did not return *The Captain Takes a Wife* to the library, as was my normal pattern. I had read the juicier parts the previous afternoon and planned to reread them later that afternoon. I spent the afternoon at the library reading a book entitled *H. M. Pulham, Esq.* I knew it was not a book that the librarian would allow me to check out, so I planned to read it in daily segments. I was so absorbed in the book that I did not realize it was getting dark outside. When the librarian advised me that it was getting late, I grabbed my selections, went through checkout, and ran all the way home. When I entered the living room, the lights were out. I felt uneasy, for the light in our living room went on at dusk and stayed on until my mother went to bed. Many of our neighbors used candles or oil lamps, but my mother scrimped and saved to keep our lights on. She was always the last one to retire after making sure that all lights were off. A light was on in the kitchen, and I ran toward it to see what was going on. Suddenly, Father loomed before me in the open kitchen door, holding high above his head *The Captain Takes a Wife*. My heart dropped to my toes. Deep trouble was staring me straight in the face. "Where did you get this book?" Father asked. Trembling with fear, I answered, "I got it from the library."

With his next question, my fear deepened. "Have you read it? How could you read this filth? Why would a library carry filth like this?" I stood before him, head down, stunned into silence.

That day, I learned how easy it is to slip into cowardice. Taking a deep breath, I blurted out that Mrs. McMillan had made me take a restricted adult card because I had read everything on the children's side. She was supposed to check the books I took out. It was all her fault. How was I to know that the book had all that filth in it? I thought it was a story about sailors. As the final touch, I laid my head on the kitchen table and burst into deep, wrenching sobs.

Both my mother and father attempted to console me. After all, I was only a child. Perhaps the librarian was at fault. I couldn't be expected to know the content of every book in the library, but she should. By God, it was her business to know!

I cannot vouch for the validity of what follows, for my brother, who made it his business to be hanging out at the library the next afternoon, reported it to me.

True to his word, Father stopped off the next day after work. When he asked to see Mrs. McMillan, she came out to greet him, wearing a broad smile. That smile quickly disappeared when she saw the scowl on his face. As the frown on his forehead deepened, she asked, "Mr. Sprague, what's wrong?"

Pulling the book from his jacket pocket, he responded, "This is what's wrong! Why would you expose my child to this filth! In fact, why would you give her a restricted adult library card without first consulting me? Look at this! Read it for yourself!"

Father had marked the racier passages of the book with cardboard markers. As Mrs. McMillan glanced down at the open page, she winced in pain. It was obvious that even she was shocked. As she later told my father, she had no idea that a book of that nature was available in the library. She apologized, profusely, and promised to hold a massive inventory to see what else might be lurking, unbidden, in Lothrop Library's book stacks.

It took some doing, but she finally calmed my father. As he turned to go, he said, "I don't know how you can straighten this out with Marvin. I'll leave it up to you to try to explain why you forced that restricted adult card on her against her will."

In strangled tones, Mrs. McMillan asked, "Is that what she told you?"

Father answered, "Of course, that's what she told me. What else could she say but the truth? After all, she's just a child. What would she know about the difference between children's books and adult books?"

Mrs. McMillan apologized, again, and then said, "Good night."

My brother said she stood looking after my father long after the door had slammed shut behind him.

The next day, I went to the library as usual. When the clerk at the counter did not say hello, I thought nothing of it. But when I passed Mrs. McMillan and she did not speak, only nodded her head, I did take notice. As usual, I took my selections to the counter for checkout. This time, the clerk examined each book in minute detail, even taking time to fan through them and silently read excerpts. Finally, she date-stamped them and handed them to me, then turned her back and walked away. I did not need to ask why everyone was acting differently. I knew.

Gradually, the number of days I visited Lothrop Library decreased. I took to reading my brother's science fiction magazines. While they were not interesting reading, the graphic sketches more than made up for the dullness of the stories. If Father thought *The Captain Takes a Wife* was filth, he should have seen the drawings of scantily clad ladies that adorned the pages of my brother's magazines. It seemed that ladies of the year 2000 would be stripped down for action—that is, action as space ship pilots.

For about a year, I existed without access to my beloved books. It was the longest year of my young life. To be separated from something you love is like having a death in the family. Father celebrated my sudden interest in reading the daily newspaper. He did not know that I was hungry for the printed word in whatever form I could find it.

By the time I was reduced to reading the labels on cereal boxes each morning at breakfast, the Master decided I had been punished enough. Word came, through the ever-faithful Beatrice, that Mrs. McMillan was no longer head librarian at Lothrop Library. The position was political, and since there had been a change of mayor, a change in head librarian had followed. The new librarian cleaned house and brought in her own people. In wiping the slate clean for herself, she had wiped the slate clean for me.

I returned to the library and secured a new restricted adult card. The new librarian was not as diligent as Mrs. McMillan. No one checked my books or challenged my selections. I was completely footloose and fancy-free, but the magic was gone. I did not regularly visit a library again until after I graduated from Sill School and was old enough to go to the main library by myself.

MISS LILA'S PLACE

It's strange how places often take on the identity of the people who occupy them. So it was with the apartment once occupied by the Saxon family. Two years after they left town, the apartment they vacated was still referred to as the Saxon apartment. At least it was until a June day in 1937 when an event occurred that forever changed the way the neighborhood identified that dark, dingy apartment.

Saturday was the only day of the week that my brother and I were allowed to sleep in. It was the day we could stay in bed until at least eight o'clock in the morning. On this particular Saturday morning, we were awakened early by the sound of a truck with its engine running and a very noisy muffler. Doors opened and slammed shut, and an unfamiliar voice barked sharp commands to someone inside the Saxon apartment. My brother and I bolted from bed and fought for access to the bathroom, because we knew our mother would not let us so much as look out of the window until we had washed up and put on clothes. After splashing my face with water, I hastily dressed, rushed to the back porch, and looked over the banister to the yard below. For a moment I gasped in amazement at the array of furnishings covering the yard in front of the Saxon apartment.

Directly across from the front entrance of the apartment stood a long, red velvet sofa. Opposite the sofa, two large, dark beige, plush armchairs waited to be occupied. Several mahogany end tables held tall, pink ceramic lamps with white silk shades, which were adorned with small velvet balls the color of the sofa. A large circular coffee table stood in the center of the yard, while an area by the back fence contained a stack of large cardboard boxes. A mattress and bedspring leaned against the solitary tree at the center of the courtyard, while the outline of a four-poster bed could be seen through the front bedroom window. An assortment of vases, figurines, china, and silverware waited to be released from their open containers. Piled by the side porch was an assortment of brooms, mops, and other cleaning materials, while a large assortment of luggage and hatboxes were scattered up and down the walkway. It was not the quantity of what I saw but the apparent newness of everything that impressed me.

I was definitely not the only one interested in what was happening at the Saxon apartment. Up and down Herbert Street, people could be seen moving from porch to porch in search of a better view of the goings on at our building. Some of the ladies idly swept the sidewalks in front of their residences while keeping a keen eye on the entrance to our front yard. Even my mother, who customarily set up her quilting frame on the front section of our porch in good weather, felt the urge to move it, temporarily, to the back side—the better to keep an eye on the bottom landing leading to the Saxon apartment.

That something unusual was afoot did not come as a complete surprise. The odor of cheap paint had hung in the air for almost a week. Workmen had been seen coming and going, and the banging of hammers was heard far into the night. It was all very puzzling. Prior to my father's arrival, no one remembered a repair being made on the building except when a building inspector, fearful of losing his job, would insist that the landlord make at least a pretense of correcting some obvious and long-standing defect. My father was a skilled carpenter and often offered to make repairs to the building in exchange for a month's rent. Since repairs made by my father fully met the city code, the landlord would quickly accept the offers.

It was when the landlord showed up one morning to monitor the work being done on the apartment that neighborhood curiosity reached fever pitch. You see, in all the years that we had lived on Herbert Street, you could count Mr. Guntz's visits to the neighborhood on the fingers of one hand. Scranton's Realty company on West Warren handled rent collections for the building. On this Saturday, it seemed our curiosity would finally be satisfied.

It was about four o'clock in the afternoon when a long black luxury sedan pulled up in front of the building. Out stepped the handsomest man I had ever seen. I had, on the day that Joe Louis visited his aunt, proclaimed Joe the handsomest man in the world, but I was soon to revise that opinion. Mr. Jones, his name was Mr. Jones, left the Brown Bomber in the shade as far as looks were concerned. People began to flood the street, openly vying for the best position to see the other occupant of the car. We didn't have to wait long. When Mr. Jones opened the passenger door out stepped a woman dressed to the hilt in the latest fashion.

Despite the obvious quality of the clothes she wore, physically she was quite plain. She was about five feet five inches tall with full breasts, slim hips, and short hair, dyed red. A wave of disappointment moved through the crowd, and Sister English was heard to say, "Why, she's nothing to write home about."

Then, she smiled. It was as though a hundred-watt bulb had clicked on inside her head, causing her eyes to glisten and deep, deep dimples to appear in her cheeks, dimples so deep that you felt the urge to stick your fingers into each side to see if they would meet in the middle. Teetering on three-inch heels, she gracefully navigated the path to the apartment. The neighborhood ladies sighed in envy at the sight of her silk-covered legs and slender ankles. The men acted as though they had not noticed her, while their wives moved closer to them as if establishing ownership rights. Only John Henry, the neighborhood drunk, mumbled, "You sure can see why he's crazy about her."

There was no response to his comment from the crowd.

Our new neighbor lost no time in introducing herself to the other occupants of the building. She seemed to have an understanding of the order of importance of each of her neighbors. Mr. Guntz had told her to consult my father, first, if she had any problems with her apartment, so her first visit was to my mother. In succeeding days she visited the Davis, Albert, and Moore families. Mother said she struck just the right note, pleasant but reserved. She found something in each house to admire, which, of course, pleased the lady of the house very much. By the time she had finished her rounds, the general consensus of the building's occupants was that Miss Lila was a real nice lady. No one mentioned her gentleman friend, who arrived every Friday and left every Sunday afternoon.

What really fascinated everyone was the fact that she had a telephone. Even the telephone installers remarked they couldn't remember the last time they had installed a private phone in our neighborhood.

During the week, Miss Lila stayed close to home, except for a weekly shopping trip on Thursday. Shortly before lunchtime, a car would arrive to transport her away on her excursion. Immaculately dressed and with every hair in place, she would wave gaily to everyone on the street while the driver would softly toot his horn to signal departure. Late that evening, the car would return dispersing first Miss Lila and then numerous boxes and bags from prominent downtown stores. Bringing up the rear would be endless bags of groceries. It was the volume of groceries that seemed to amaze my mother. Each Thursday she would comment, as if for the first time, "She buys enough groceries to feed an army."

At the height of the depression, such abundance was unheard of. Oddly

JEFFERSON PUBLIC LIBRARY
321 S. Main Street
Jefferson, WI 53549
·674-7733

enough, Miss Lila's lifestyle only enhanced the neighborhood's admiration of her. With the exception of some members of the Church of the True Believers, most people were proud to claim her as a neighbor.

On Friday evenings, if the weather was warm, we would hear the plaintive wail of the latest blues recordings wafting through Miss Lila's open windows. In the breaks between playing recordings, Mr. Jones's booming laugh could be heard. Occasionally, you could catch the echo of Miss Lila's gentle laughter and her soft voice as she asked, "Jonsie, would you like some chicken? Aren't you going to try some of the ham? I fixed the green beans and white potatoes just for you. Don't you want some? Would you rather have sweet potato pie or chocolate cake?"

The list of prepared foods would go on and on with Mr. Jones accepting or rejecting at will.

Among the people who overheard these conversations, there was one hotly debated question. Did Miss Lila really prepare all the foods she mentioned? There was no middle ground. You either believed every word she said, or you believed that she was lying to impress the neighborhood. While my father had an opinion, everyone did not share it.

On the morning of the second Monday after Miss Lila's arrival, she was observed calling several of the neighborhood children to her door. Mrs. Eubanks just happened to be sitting at her front room window and saw the entire goings on. She later said, "I sat there for more than an hour before I figured out what she was doing. She would give each child a brown paper bag and they would head off in the direction of their home. Finally, it was the careful way they handled the bag that made me think it was something very precious. I couldn't think of anything more precious to their families than food."

As usual, Mrs. Eubanks had used her plain common sense to solve a problem. Miss Lila was sharing her leftover food with the poorest families in the neighborhood. Each family had been given an array of leftovers from her weekend cooking. There were portions of chicken, steak, green beans, white potatoes, squash, slices of ham, sweet potato pie, double chocolate cake, and lemon meringue pie—the remains of her offerings to Mr. Jones. When she learned what the paper bags contained, Mrs. Eubanks just laughed and said, "I told you to listen to Mr. Sprague when he said, 'I'll bet you money I don't have that, if she says she has it, she has it.'"

For my mother, it was not the contents of the bags that impressed her but the gracious way they were offered. Miss Lila included a note in each bag asking that the family help her out in honoring her mother's mandate to "Waste not, want

JEFFERSON PUBLIC LIBRARY
121 S. Main Street
Jackson, MT 55840
679-7733

not." To throw good food in the garbage was sinful, and she said that she hoped they would help her to avoid committing a sin. Mother's favorite saying was "Take from no bird her song," and in Miss Lila she had found a kindred spirit.

The following week when Miss Lila asked my mother to alter two dresses for her, she accepted immediately. I was overjoyed because my prayers had been answered. I, like everyone else in the neighborhood, was possessed by a burning desire to see the inside of Miss Lila's apartment. My dream was about to come true.

Aunt Bessie described what followed as the strangest thing she had ever seen. My mother spent many hours visiting Miss Lila. While some of this time was spent in altering and hemming the continuous array of new frocks purchased by Miss Lila, most of it was spent in conversations, which were always held at a voice level too low for me to catch more than a few words or phrases. It didn't matter. I was so fascinated by the furnishings in the apartment that my natural curiosity was stilled. They looked like something out of the movies shown at the Rogers and Beechwood Theaters. If I had not been so enthralled in investigating the many pictures and plaques that dotted the walls, I would have wondered at my mother's listening, with obvious enjoyment, to recordings by Bessie Smith, Muddy Waters, and someone named Wild Dog Harris.

My natural curiosity may have been derailed but not that of the neighborhood. Even my mother's closest friends began to question why she was spending so much time at Miss Lila's. Father, after coming home on several occasions to an empty house and cold skillets, asked, "Why do you have to spend so much time there? You've done a lot of alterations, but the people have always come to you. What's so special about her?" My mother did not respond but continued preparing a late supper.

It was Aunt Bessie who finally defended my mother to my father and members of the church congregation. When the questions were raised to her, she simply replied, "Why, it should be perfectly clear what Sister Sprague is doing. She's obviously holding Bible studies with Miss Lila. I wouldn't be surprised to see Miss Lila march down the center aisle of the church any Sunday."

Momentarily, her comments seemed to still the raging beast, but she and Mother both knew it would rear its ugly head again. My aunt cautioned my mother that her frequent visits to Miss Lila's would have to stop. My mother replied, "I know you're right, Bessie, but I seem to have lost control. I do enjoy her company more than any other women except you. She's a good woman, and she really loves Mr. Jones. It's a shame they didn't meet before he married."

Aunt Bessie gathered up her purse and turned to leave. At the door, she turned and said, "Gracie, remember you're the one who told me, 'The Devil's a busy man.' "

Mother cringed as the door closed behind my aunt.

Mother did decrease the number and length of her visits but not enough for anyone to notice. I wondered how it would all end, but I need not have worried. Reverend Elder was right. The Lord takes care of his own.

One Friday afternoon, in the spring of the next year, the black Lincoln did not appear. Several people commented that it was the first weekend that Mr. Jones had failed to show. There were even some unflattering comments along the lines of "Maybe he's getting tired of her. You know these fancy women wear out after a while."

Such comments quickly ended as the majority of the women rushed to Miss Lila's defense. As the conversation turned to other matters, Miss Lila and her missing gentleman friend dropped from mind.

Early the next morning, the neighborhood was awakened by loud screams coming from Miss Lila's apartment. While I rushed to the spot on the balcony that overlooked her front door, my mother ran down to the apartment and banged on the door screaming, "Lila, what's wrong? What's wrong?" Finally, the door opened, and my mother went in, closing the door behind her.

Suddenly, I began to shake as I remembered standing at this same spot while my mother spoke to Mrs. Saxon about her husband, Reverend Saxon. As William rushed up beside me, I pushed those unpleasant thoughts from my mind. My brother, as was true of most of the males in the area, adored Miss Lila. In her presence, he stood ramrod straight, ever on the ready to assist her in any way possible.

Finally, my mother came out carrying a large bag in her hand. She brushed past the people gathered in front of Miss Lila's house and went up the steps where my father waited. In a low voice, she said something to him. Then, drying her eyes on the corner of her apron, she went into her bedroom and closed the door. My father said, "You children be quiet; your mother doesn't feel well."

The next day, the black sedan arrived pulling a trailer behind it. The driver was a stranger to us. He, and two other men, hastily filled the trailer with cartons, small articles of furniture, and numerous suitcases and hatboxes. Finally, Miss Lila emerged dressed totally in black. She was wearing the black dress my mother had taken from her house on Saturday and worked feverishly overnight to alter. She wore a wide-brimmed, black nylon hat with a long sheer veil completely covering her face. She silently embraced my mother, then got into the car and was driven off. Just as with Reverend Saxon, she was never seen again.

When the Detroit edition of the *Chicago Defender* newspaper came out that Wednesday, the lead story was of a gangland shooting in Chicago on the preceding Friday. There, staring at us from front-page center, was a faded picture of Mr. Jones. A rival number's kingpin had killed him. The article stated, "He left to mourn him a wife and four children, as well as numerous other relatives and friends." As my father read the list of mourners out loud, my mother added, "And Miss Lila."

Nearly a month later, a package arrived in the mail addressed to my mother. We all held our breath as she slowly unwrapped it to reveal four records. Immediately, I recognized them as the recordings that Miss Lila would play on lazy summer afternoons. As my mother held them in her hands, tears began to form in her eyes. My father patted her on the shoulder, took the records, and placed them in the center drawer of the chifforobe. My brother and I looked at each other with wide eyes because only very special articles found their way to that center drawer.

Some people create a lasting impression. In less than a year, Miss Lila had made that dark, dingy little apartment hers, forever. Long after the people who knew her had died or moved away, it was still referred to as Miss Lila's place.

MY BROTHER AND THE
KATZENJAMMER KIDS

The few months Miss Lila spent with us made a tremendous impression on my brother. At the age of fourteen, he had discovered the opposite sex. Father could hardly contain his joy as my brother moped around like a lovesick puppy. I heard Father tell my mother that he didn't want William to be a sex maniac, but he did want him to at least notice the difference between the sexes. Mother's response was so low as to be indiscernible. Even at the age of ten, I realized that Mother was uncomfortable discussing sexual matters. When I began to ask the basic birds-and-bees questions, she sent me to Aunt Bessie for the answers. As the years passed, I began to appreciate my mother's wisdom in directing me to my aunt.

After Miss Lila left, the relationship between my father and brother underwent a change. They began to take long walks, from which I was excluded. They held deep conversations, which my brother, when questioned, would describe as "nothing." Change was in the air, and not all of it was negative.

My brother began to rebel against taking me everywhere with him. Although Mother would insist that he let me go along with him on trips to the store or to the playground, Father would override her and send him off alone. This suited me just fine. I was sick of playing tag-a-long and was very happy to travel the highways and byways with my friends. Finally, Mother conceded defeat, and my brother was left to his own devices.

William was an egghead. All he required to keep him happy was a stack of science fiction magazines and a book of mathematical puzzles. He loved music and played the violin. It was the violin only because Mr. Kraus, the shoe cobbler, had traded my father a violin for a set of handmade cabinets. Since he was teaching his son, Julius, to play the violin, Mr. Kraus allowed my brother to sit in on the lessons for free. The screeching and wailing drove my mother to distraction until she finally banished his practice sessions to the selfsame coal shed that had played such an infamous part in the Reverend Saxon affair. There, William could practice the violin to his heart's content.

Gradually, his playing improved to the point that Mother began to enjoy it. Fortunately, that point was reached well before the first frost, and winter found him practicing in the dining room to loud applause. My brother seemed at peace in his world until the Katzenjammer Kids appeared on the scene.

Although the neighborhood children had the usual number of falling outs and threatened fisticuffs, they got along reasonably well. Occasionally, a disagreement would lead to a physical fight. Such fights were rare, because when they were reported to the parents of the participants by some well-meaning observer, retribution followed hard and fast. Most parents were pushing for a better way of life for their offspring, and time wasted in fighting was not considered a part of that push. That is why the entrance of the Katzenjammer Kids came as such a shock to the neighborhood.

Of course, their name was not really Katzenjammer Kids but the Neal boys. Father borrowed the name from a popular comic strip that featured a bunch of scruffy ragamuffins who excelled at getting into mischief. Although it was a comic strip, it did not appeal to most children. We leaned heavily toward Dick Tracy, Flash Gordon, Tarzan, Buck Rogers, and Little Orphan Annie. Father, however, found the Kids hilarious. Every Sunday, we had to wait until he had finished reading the Katzenjammer Kids before we were allowed to look at the comics.

The newspaper was my father's only obsession. In difficult times, he would give up tailor-made suits, leather-soled shoes, even the occasional pack of Camel cigarettes but never his copy of the *Detroit Times*. Although Father's reference to the Neal boys as the Katzenjammer Kids was made in passing, the name stuck.

The Neal family moved into the little house on the alley in the summer of 1938. Word had it that they had been literally run off the east side. Mr. Woodruff, who had a cousin living on Riopelle Street, said the neighborhood grew so weary of the problems they created that they had physically packed them up and sent them on their way. They moved into the little house because it was the only vacant housing that the welfare department could locate on such short notice. It was the talk of the neighborhood. How in the world could seven people live in three small rooms? That question was never answered, because in the ten months they lived there, no one was ever invited into their home.

At first, the brothers seemed no worse than several other bullies in the neighborhood. The four of them delighted in teasing and threatening smaller children, but nothing physical resulted. They were large for their ages, eleven through fourteen, and were at least two years behind in their school grades. They attended school only occasionally, and the truant officer soon gave up on them.

Mrs. Neal and her two daughters stayed close to home. Mr. Neal, if he existed, was never seen. Every other Thursday, when the welfare check arrived, the mother and daughters would emerge from their house and take the bus downtown. They'd return that afternoon laden with bags labeled Sam's Cut Rate Department Store, Mary Ann's Shoes, and Kresge's Five-and-Dime. On summer evenings, they would sit on their small front stoop dressed in all of their newly acquired finery. When I asked Aunt Bessie why they only wore their new clothes once, she answered, "Baby, those clothes are so cheap that once they're washed, they don't look new anymore."

It was after school started in the fall that I first noticed the change in my brother. Always the last to arrive home from school, suddenly he was always there when I arrived. It seemed that instead of walking home from Northwestern High School, he would take the bus. I was surprised because he had always walked in order to save his bus fare to buy his precious science fiction magazines. He said he liked to walk because it gave him time to think. It was Beatrice who alerted me to the real reason that he was in such a hurry to get home.

The Katzenjammer Kids were hounding him. It seemed it had started during the summer. At first, he said he didn't think much about it, because in a fair fight, he knew he could whip any one of the Neal boys. It was when they threatened to gang up on him that he began to worry. He didn't want to tell Father, yet he knew that he could not defend himself against what amounted to a mob. He couldn't talk to Uncle Smitty about it because he certainly would have spilled the beans. He was definitely on the horns of a dilemma.

William returned from school earlier and earlier each day. I was certain he was cutting his last class in an effort to avoid the Neal boys. Sometimes he arrived at our front door out of breath as if he had been chased home. Although he tried to appear unconcerned, I could see that the tension and apprehension were wearing him down. More importantly, it was having the same effect on me. Finally, I could stand it no longer. One evening, when my brother was at Mr. Kraus's taking a violin lesson, I poured my heart out to Father. My confession was brought on when Father asked, "You've been awfully quiet lately, is something wrong?"

The floodgates opened. All the fear and apprehension I had been feeling over the past few months rushed out in a torrent of words that bordered on hysteria.

Throwing myself on Father, I said, "The Neal boys are going to kill William! He never did anything to them! They're just big bullies, and William doesn't want to tell you because you say we have to fight our own battles! Please, don't tell William I told you!"

It took a while for my father to quiet me down. When I finally stopped crying, out of sheer exhaustion, he said, "You did right to tell me. We don't want your brother to know that I know. Don't worry. No one is going to kill your brother."

That night, as I lay in bed reading the Five Little Peppers and How They Grew by flashlight, I heard Father and Mother discussing the situation. They had left their bedroom door open to catch what little breeze came in from the open dining room window, and their voices carried in the still calm of the hot summer night. I did not understand everything they said, but the words William, bullies, and Neal family came through clearly.

The next day was Saturday. It was time for Father's weekly visit to Campbell's Cleaners. The shop was both a cleaners and a gathering place for the men in the neighborhood. It was located on the corner of McGraw and Scotten. Since McGraw Street was a block north of West Warren, the cleaners lay well beyond our assigned boundary. The restriction against crossing Warren Avenue was not because it led to an undesirable neighborhood but because Warren Avenue was considered the great dividing line between the haves and the have-nots on the west side of town. Our street lay on the wrong side of that magic line.

The Saturday morning gatherings at Campbell's Cleaners assembled many of the brightest minds in the area. Doctors, lawyers, and ministers rubbed shoulders with waiters, construction workers, dishwashers, and hustlers. Many a far-reaching family decision was born at these weekly assemblies. You would always find my father in the midst of the fray as those in attendance waited for whatever words of wisdom he chose to dispense. That week was different as Father anxiously awaited the group's approval of a solution he proposed to the Katzenjammer Kids problem. Uncle Smitty later told Mother that the group had concurred in his proposal with minor adjustments. Although I listened at every door, I did not hear even a hint of what that solution might be.

In the following weeks, little appeared to change. My brother still arrived home from school early, and Father appeared unconcerned about it. It became obvious that the Kids were increasing the pressure on my brother. Mother often saw them chasing William around the corner of Bangor and Herbert Streets as he pushed himself to home and safety. I had never seen my mother angry before. She always seemed to be able to find a reason, an excuse, for even the most hideous behavior. Father often said, "Gracie, you take this forgiving thing too far!"

This was a different woman. She was beyond anger and had moved on to rage. It took all of Father's persuasion to prevent her from storming the Neal house and physically assaulting both the boys and their mother. Father was so alarmed that he sent for Reverend Elder. The Reverend came and prayed with my mother, but you could still see the anger bubbling up in her eyes. Over and over again, Father tried to reassure her that he had everything under control and that the situation would be resolved, shortly.

It was on a Friday afternoon that things came to a climax. Father came home early from work. He told my mother that he just had a feeling that this might be the day. As the time for my brother to arrive home came and went, he began to pace the yard in front of our steps. Finally, we saw my brother come around the corner in full flight from the Neal boys. Usually, they would stop chasing him about midway down the block, but when they looked up and saw Father standing on the steps, you could see the decision to change their strategy take shape in their eyes. They increased their pace and arrived at the bottom of our steps hard on my brother's heels. Gasping for breath, they looked up at Father as if daring him to say or do anything.

Father leaned back against the banister. He seemed completely at ease. William stood at his side with an uncertain look on his face. He started to say something, but Father gestured with his hand for him to shut up. He closed his mouth as directed, and the silence that ensued seemed to go on forever. Mother and I stood in the front door, watching. Father seemed unaware of our presence as he fixed his gaze on Milton Neal, the oldest of the Katzenjammer Kids. Finally, he broke the silence.

"Hi, Milton, what's going on? Why are you chasing my boy? What has he done to you?"

Milton dug his toe into the dry dirt at the bottom of the steps, hung his head, and said nothing. The silence resumed as if it had never been broken. Finally, aware of the restless movements of his younger brothers, who stood in a semicircle behind him, Milton forced out, "We're chasing him because we want to, that's why."

Folding and unfolding his arms, Father replied, "I don't think so. Now if William and you have a problem, then you need to sit down and discuss it. If you can't settle it by talking, then maybe you ought to put on some gloves and duke it out. You will not, however, gang up on him and beat him up just because you want to."

I knew by the expression on Milton's face that he had never been challenged before. He didn't know what to do. It was obvious, however, from the movements of his brothers that he had to do something soon. Taking his courage in hand, he said, "We'll beat him up anytime we want to. What can you do about it? There's four of us and only two of you."

My father smiled at him in satisfaction and said, "But you see, that's where you make your mistake. This isn't really about me and my son, or you and your brothers. It's about you and me. I'm not going to hold your brothers responsible for anything that happens to my boy. From this day forward, if William stumbles and falls, I will come looking for you. If anyone takes it into his or her head to beat him up, I will seek you out. You'd better pray to your God that nothing happens to him while you're living in this neighborhood, because it will rest on your head."

That day, I learned the meaning of the expression "divide and conquer." Even before my father had finished speaking, the other Neal boys were slowly backing up, putting space between themselves and their brother. As Milton looked around at his disappearing brothers, a look of absolute terror settled on his face. Father stood as if etched in stone, staring directly into his eyes. Finally, Milton unlocked his legs and slowly, at first, and then with increasing speed, followed his brothers out of the gate and down the street. By the time he reached the corner of Bangor and Herbert, he was lost in a cloud of dust.

It was the next evening that Reverend Elder came by to tell my parents that Mrs. Neal had come to the church to ask for help in pressuring social services to find her family a larger house in a different neighborhood. The Reverend had talked to one of the Scranton brothers about the situation. They owned the Scranton Realty office at the corner of Scotten and Warren. The problem of the Neal family was not completely new to Mr. Scranton, for he was convinced that the Neal brothers had performed the acts of vandalism his business had suffered since their arrival in the area. He told Reverend Elder not to worry. He would contact the social worker and work with her to find a rental property as far away from our neighborhood as possible. He soon located a house in Inkster, Michigan, and in less than two weeks, the Neals were gone.

The weekend after they moved, the church held a barbecue. Reverend severely chastised those members who suggested that it was held in celebration of the Neal family's departure. She claimed that the barbecue had been planned for months. The church secretary kept her mouth shut but later told my mother that she could not find the barbecue listed anywhere on the Church calendar.

There was, however, no uncertainty regarding the report that Mrs. Eubanks had informed her sister-in-law in Inkster of the pending arrival of the Neal family.

It was the Christian thing to do.

WHAT'S IN A NAME?

Everything! It was not until I reached the fourth grade that I learned just how important a name could be. I gained this knowledge through an encounter with a new boy at school named Tommy Armstrong. He had recently moved to Detroit from New York and was determined to establish himself as the head honcho of the fourth grade class of Sill School. He soon discovered that the only way to success lay through an affiliation with Marvin Sprague.

He tried to curry favor in the only way he knew. He tormented me. After trying the usual attention-getting mechanisms of hair pulling and name calling, and receiving only that universal response of "Sticks and stones may break my bones, but names will never hurt me," he turned ugly. Tommy Armstrong failed to understand that I was totally ignorant of the rules of conduct for social inter-course between the sexes. While some of my girlfriends were beginning to expand their horizons to include mild flirtations with their male counterparts, Beatrice and I were still playing stickball and building skateboards. The only boys that interested us were the ones who would share their knowledge of how to fix a broken skate with a rusty nail.

In desperation, Tommy flung out what he considered to be the coup de grâce, he called me "four eyes." Much to his amazement, I did not react. I had recently been fitted with what were perhaps the ugliest eyeglasses in the known world, so it was not surprising that he believed a reference to them would be a crushing blow. Ugly they were, but more importantly, they opened up new vistas for me. The optometrist told my father that I had probably been visually impaired since birth. My glasses were my most precious possession. They were the first thing I put on in the morning and the last thing I took off at night. Tommy's slur on my glasses only cemented my dislike for him.

Like most bullies, Tommy Armstrong could not stand to be ignored, and to be ignored by a mere girl was unthinkable. Then, one day, in idle conversation, he hit on the one thing that pushed my panic button. He said, "Marvin's got a boy's name!"

I cannot truthfully say that I had no inkling of the masculinity of my name. Over the years, people had mentioned that they knew men with the name Marvin. When I had questioned my mother on the subject, she had responded that I was named for my spiritual godmother, Marvin Taylor, who had died shortly before my birth. Thereafter, when queried about the gender of my name, I mentioned being named for my godmother, and it ended there. This time, however, the questions continued. In desperation, I again questioned my mother about the origination of my name only to be assured that my name could apply to either a man or a woman. My aunt was present during this conversation but did not join in the discussion. This was unusual, for my mother always said that Aunt Bessie was far better at explaining things to my brother and me than she would ever be.

It was the next day that my mother suggested I spend the weekend with Aunt Bessie. Uncle Chuck had returned to his job on the railroad, and it was lonely rattling around in that big, old house. As Aunt Bessie and I left our house, Mother came to the door and said, "Have a good time, Marvin." Then, turning to my aunt, she said, "Thanks, Bessie, I'll never be able to repay you."

Aunt Bessie smiled, and we continued down the walkway and out the gate.

That night, as we munched on popcorn and listened to the Saturday Night Hit Parade, my aunt told me the story of Marvin Taylor, the woman whose name I carried.

My mother was born in 1894 to parents who were unusually old to be starting a family. Her mother, Alice Lewis, was thirty-four years old when she was born, and her father, Elisha Lewis, celebrated his thirty-eighth birthday within one week of her birth. Most married people of that generation were grandparents by their age. Both had been previously married, then widowed, without being blessed with children. Although they had always wanted children, they viewed the late arrival of my mother and her sister, Margaret, as a mixed blessing. Years of farming had weakened them physically, and just as they looked forward to slowing down and enjoying life, up popped two daughters. Since they believed that all things happen for God's own purpose, they girded their loins and did the best they could.

It soon became evident that my mother, although the first born, was not first in her mother's heart. Try as she might, Grandma Alice could not hide the special affection she held for her youngest daughter, Margaret, who not only looked like her but also walked, talked, and thought like her. In short, they were as alike as two peas in a pod. My mother was left to the ministrations of her father, who willingly shared with her his most prized possession, his love of books. My grandfather was a learned man. The only son of a wealthy tobacco farmer and a young female slave, he had been taught to read and write at an early age.

Years later, this ability proved to be his oldest daughter's salvation. Buried in one of the numerous books that lined the walls of their small farmhouse, my mother could feel as wanted, loved, and cherished as she chose to be.

When Mother's parents decided to send Margaret to college instead of my mother, despite the fact that my mother was the oldest and had long professed a strong desire to attend university, it was the straw that broke the camel's back. In truth, the decision was actually made by grandmother, but grandfather agreed with her for the sake of peace.

That day, Mother wrote to her friend Bessie Sims, my aunt Bessie, who had left the small town of Berry, Kentucky, to find work in Chicago, Illinois, and had never returned. Later, she had married and moved to St. Louis, Missouri. Mother considered Bessie as more of a sister than Margaret. I saw Aunt Margaret so seldom in my lifetime that I never thought of her as a relative. Mother seldom mentioned her name. Within two weeks, Mother was on her way to join Bessie in St. Louis with the dire admonitions of her mother still ringing in her ears.

In St. Louis my mother soon found work at a local women's apparel shop, Lowe's Emporium. Skilled in fine needlework, she was immediately assigned to hand-finishing special orders placed by society ladies. News soon circulated among Lowe's customers concerning the new Negro girl who had such a beautiful touch with embroidery. One by one, the ladies found their way to the Phillis Wheatley Home for Young Ladies, where my mother lived.

When the manager of the dressmaking department at Lowe's Emporium found out that some of his customers were making direct contact with Grace Lewis, he called her into his office. Although my mother had been raised to be a lady, she had a backbone of steel and did not hesitate to stand up for herself. When the manager saw his threats were in vain, he caved in and advised her to set up a business on the side. He even drew up a price list for her, telling her not to give her work away too cheaply. She did beautiful work, and the society ladies could well afford to pay her fairly for it. For a while she continued to do consignment work for Lowe's, but eventually the sheer volume of her outside work overtook her, and she and Lowe's went their separate ways. She never forgot the manager, Mr. Link. She always said he was one of the fairest men she had ever known.

About the time my mother quit working for Lowe's, a young lady from Philadelphia moved into the Phillis Wheatley home. Her arrival created quite a stir. She was simply the most beautiful Negro girl anyone had ever seen. Of course, she was snubbed by most of the other young ladies in the building but not by my mother and Bessie. Mother had not forgotten how fortunate she had been to have her friend Bessie run interference for her when she first arrived in St. Louis, frightened and alone. Together, they took the new girl, Marvin Simpson, to their bosom and helped her through the initial shock of leaving home and family to find her way in the world. Thus, the stage was set for a three-way friendship that was to last for as long as they lived.

Marvin worked as a nurse's assistant at the St. Louis General Hospital. She had taken a nursing course in Philadelphia and had graduated with top honors. Unable to find a position at home, even with outstanding credentials, she had answered an ad in the local paper offering positions as nursing assistants at several hospitals in the St. Louis area. She had accepted an offer, and here she was, ready to start her nursing career.

When people asked why such a beautiful girl had the name Marvin, she would answer, "When I was born, the doctor told my parents that my mother could not have any more babies. It was too dangerous, and another birth might well kill her. My father, shaken by the news but determined to have a child named after him, named me Marvin, saying, 'I don't care if she is a girl. Her name is Marvin, and that's that!' "

When Aunt Bessie tried to describe how beautiful Marvin was, she seemed at a loss for words. Finally, she laughed and said, "One day, a man looking back at her walked into a tree and knocked himself unconscious. Now you've got to admit that she must have been a real beauty."

I snuggled down on the sofa closer to her and eagerly awaited the next installment of the Marvin Simpson story. My name was becoming more precious to me by the minute.

Marvin was beautiful but shy. She refused all dates and immersed herself in her work, often sending away for mail order lessons to update her nursing skills. That is, she refused all dates until Billy Taylor asked her to attend a Sunday afternoon church concert. To the complete surprise of my mother and aunt, she accepted the invitation. My mother was very excited. Billy Taylor worked as a maintenance man at the same hospital as Marvin and was very tall and good looking. Bessie seemed a good deal less pleased and said, "I wonder what that Billy Taylor is up to."

My mother's enthusiasm was overpowering and gradually washed away my aunt's misgivings. Both my mother and aunt were to remember those misgivings in the years to come.

After their first date, the die was cast. The plot developed rapidly. In fact, too rapidly, my aunt was heard to say. But who can remain negative in the face of true love. Marvin took Billy back to Philadelphia on vacation, and her family and friends placed the stamp of approval on the relationship. They returned from vacation engaged and already preparing for a lavish wedding the next June. Everyone agreed it was a good match. Marvin was beautiful and had a good job. Billy was handsome and was considered a sort of jackleg supervisor over the cleaning staff at the hospital. All in all, it seemed a very satisfactory state of affairs. Only my aunt remained silent on the subject.

All that winter, my mother worked on Marvin's wedding gown. It was an original creation, lavish with hand embroidery, lace overlays, and crocheted rosettes. Mr. Link contributed a bag of lace remnants from a cutting of party dresses at Lowe's, and several of the dressmakers still working there came by with remnants that were far larger than a remnant should be. When queried, they all swore that Mr. Link had approved them as scraps so they could be used in good conscience. As the date approached, Marvin's mother came to town to assist in the final preparations.

The wedding was to be held at the Phillis Wheatley home. Marvin's mother wanted the wedding to take place in Philadelphia, but my mother and aunt convinced her that it would be helpful to the young couple to have the wedding in the city they would live in. Finally, she gave in. Family members and friends formed a cortege and drove up to attend the wedding.

The wedding day dawned warm and fair. It was a picture-perfect day. The staircase of the home was draped with pink and white roses, and vases of pink roses surrounded the borrowed altar in the living room. There wasn't a spare inch of floor space as the happy couple vowed to love, honor, and obey for as long as they both shall live.

As Aunt Bessie emptied the second bowl of popcorn, she said, "Marvin, it's getting late. What if I save the rest of the story for tomorrow?"

It took a moment for the question to register. I had become so involved in the story that reality had faded, and I was standing in that living room in St. Louis, listening to Marvin and Billy repeat their vows. My aunt, knowing how sharply the tale would descent into darkness, was trying to create a gap between the pleasant part of the story and the sad portion yet to come. When she realized how deeply I was involved in the story, she reluctantly agreed to finish it that night if I would promise to sleep late the next morning. Promise made, she sat down and took up the story again.

Although few knew it, the trouble between Marvin and Billy started immediately. Billy physically abused Marvin. He was both experienced and clever. He made sure to strike Marvin on parts of her body that would be covered with clothing, never on her face or arms. When friends noticed her walking stiffly, as if in pain, they secretly joked that you could always tell a newlywed by the way they moved. Only Aunt Bessie commented that she had seen many a newlywed but none showed the effects of married life in quite that way. Gradually, Marvin and Billy were forgotten as a new wedding was in the making, the wedding of my mother and father.

Father often complained that during the winter before the Taylor wedding, he and my mother attended very few social engagements. He would grudgingly say, "Your mother was always working on that damn wedding dress."

Aunt Bessie would respond, "You should thank God for that wedding dress, Bill. Those long winter evenings you spent with Grace while she worked on that dress did more to cement your relationship than anything else."

Father would laugh but did not disagree. It was the many winter evenings that my mother and father spent together, sharing experiences, hopes, and dreams, that caused their friendship to deepen into love.

While my parents' wedding was not as fancy as the Taylor wedding, most people said it was sweeter. Aunt Bessie said that was because my father was older and understood what an undeserved kindness God had shown him by sending my young and beautiful mother to be his bride.

The marriage was blessed with three children—my brother, William, my sister, Jewel, and me. When Aunt Bessie and Uncle Chuck moved to Detroit, my parents packed their belongings and followed. Uncle Smitty found a job for my father, and my mother's skills were fully transferable. As long as there were rich society women who filled their empty days vying with each other for the title of best dressed, her skills would be in demand.

On their first Christmas Day in Detroit, someone knocked on the door. When Father went to answer, Marvin Taylor fell through the doorway and into his arms. She lay unconscious at his feet. When the city doctor arrived, he examined her, then angrily turned to my parents and asked, "Who beat this woman? She's been beaten within an inch of her life!"

Father hastened to explain the circumstances of her arrival, and the doctor calmed down. "I don't know who did this," he said, "but they need to be stomped to death. I have never seen anything like this in my life. It's a wonder she made it this far."

After the doctor left, Father turned to Mother and said, "I know who did this, that bastard Billy! I told you he was a no good son-of-a-bitch. It's a shame that Marvin has to go through this to prove it."

Mother filled a basin with warm water and sent Father to buy a jar of petroleum jelly. After stuffing her apron pockets with soft, clean rags, she entered the bedroom where Marvin lay and closed the door.

It was weeks before Marvin felt well enough to sit up. It was additional weeks before she was strong enough to take short walks from the apartment to the corner of Beaubien and St. Antoine. Gradually, she recovered and regained a measure of that famed beauty that had first attracted Billy Taylor. My mother had contacted Marvin's family and assured them she was in safe hands. She was shocked when Marvin's mother said that Billy had explained the situation to them, and they were surprised that Marvin had left Billy. All couples had these little misunderstandings. They were a part of life. Her mother even said, "It's worth having a tiff. Making up is such fun."

It was obvious that con man, Billy, had persuaded them that Marvin was in the wrong and he was in the right. Somehow, he found out Marvin was staying at our house and flooded her with pretty cards, begging letters, and protestations of undying love. Never in any of this did he admit any wrongdoing on his part, only that he was willing to forgive her, willing to take her back as if nothing had happened.

Both my mother and father begged Marvin not to return to Billy. They promised her she could live with them for as long as need be. Nurse's assistants were in high demand. She would have no difficulty finding a job. She could build a good life in Detroit. Father told her that there were plenty of good men in the world, and women as beautiful as she was could pick and choose. Marvin agreed with all they said but continued to read Billy's cards and letters.

One morning, my mother went to the market and returned to find Marvin gone. She had left a note on the kitchen table thanking my father and mother for their help. She promised to write soon. She was sure Billy was sorry for what he had done and everything would turn out for the best. My mother said that as she read the note, she felt me turning over and over in her womb. That note was the last word my parents had of Marvin for many months.

The months went by, but still no news of Marvin. Mother wrote her family, but they had not heard from her. It was as though she and Billy had dropped off the face of the earth. It was shortly before my birth that Mother received a letter from Marvin's mother conveying the sad news that Marvin was dead, beaten to death by Billy Taylor.

Aunt Bessie held me tight as I sobbed inconsolably. I don't know how I could feel the loss of someone I had never known, but I did. Consumed by a grief I could not understand, I sobbed on and on into the night. Finally, I fell asleep. I slept into the early afternoon of the next day.

When I arrived home late Sunday evening, my mother had supper waiting for me. I ate in silence as I wrestled with the question that filled both head and heart. Finally, I blurted out, "Mama, why did you name me after Marvin Taylor?"

As if she had been waiting for that question all of her life, my mother replied, "When Marvin was beaten to death, I thought my heart would break. When you were born soon after, I wanted to believe that it was God's way of giving Marvin back to me. I named you Marvin because I hoped that you would grow up to be as fine and honest a person as Marvin Taylor."

On that Sunday evening, all negative feelings regarding my name evaporated. I wore my name proudly, telling all that questioned its gender about my god-mother, Marvin Taylor, that beautiful, warm, generous spirit my mother had loved with all her heart.

THE RACE MAN

My father was a "race man," a man as loyal to his race as to his God. He believed in the Negro race—right or wrong. Unfortunately, the decades of the 1920s, 1930s, and 1940s provided an abundance of slurs and injustices directed at members of our race. Our neighborhood was a mixture of Negro, Indian, Hungarian, and Polish families, with a smidgen of middle class Jewish tradesmen and their families. Since most of the battles my father waged were between the have-nots and the "system," and not between black and white, they were of interest to the majority of residents in the area.

His effort to increase his children's feelings of self worth was most apparent in his approach to child rearing. Every year, without fail, he would retell the story of how important my birth was to the entire country. "Times were really tough in this country in 1928," he would say. "Then, word got out that you were on the way. There was so much excitement in the news that the country began celebrating your birthday four days early, and that's how the Fourth of July holiday was born."

Mother would laugh and admonish my father, "William, stop filling Marvin's head with that foolishness. She might believe it."

Mother was right. For many years I did believe, and in a way I still do.

While my father fought racial injustice on many fronts, his major focus was directed at the racial inequities common in the public school system. Like most Negro parents in the 1930s and 1940s, he believed the road to a better life for his children ran straight through the Detroit public school system. The principal at Sill School knew him well, as he would not hesitate to take a day off from work to make the trip to Herbert and Thirtieth Streets to personally discuss some real, or imagined, wrong.

The first of Father's epic battles with the school system, that I remember, involved a home economic assignment. Although it happened more that sixty years ago, I can still recall the incident.

It began when I was reassigned from an overcrowded sewing class to a home economics class. My mother, an expert seamstress, could hardly hide her disappointment on learning of the change in class assignment. For over a year, she had carefully saved her choicest lengths of material for me to use in my sewing projects. When she saw how disappointed I was, she attempted to hide her own feelings and console me by saying, "It's all right, Baby. You'll take it next semester, and meanwhile I'll show you some beginner's sewing tips that should make it easier for you when you do take the class."

Not only did Mother console me with words but she also let me help with the preparation of the evening meals. This was a great honor as the kitchen was my mother's private domain, off-limits to everyone during business hours. Gradually, I forgot my disappointment over the change in class assignment and actually began to look forward to the home economics class.

When Mother asked how things went on my first day in class, I answered her with the question that had been puzzling me all day. "Why were the Negro students the only ones assigned to wash windows and mop floors?"

I will never forget the look that passed across my mother's face. Immediately, she responded, "Don't tell your father about your assignment."

My mother asked who was teaching the class. When told that the class was being taught by a new teacher, she said, "Oh, that explains it. She hasn't met your father, yet."

I kept my promise not to mention the incident to my father but to no avail. Unfortunately, there were few, if any, secrets in our neighborhood. Although I held my peace, my classmate Ruby told her mother, and she, in turn, told my father. As news of the incident raced through the neighborhood, anticipation of the next day's events rose to fever pitch. All who knew my father knew he would willingly take up the gauntlet.

Everyone in the neighborhood was up bright and early the next morning, even the old ladies, who normally slept until noon. The effect of their early morning rising would not be felt until the next day. Responsible for maintaining the late night vigils guaranteed to safeguard the neighborhood from peril, they would be too tired to maintain their normal schedule of midnight to dawn. For this one night, the late night travelers would not see the tattered lace curtains move in the front room windows of the nearest self-appointed guardian of the night.

Many of the neighborhood men changed their route to the bus stops in order to pass by our house to give Father the handshake of fellowship. Events of this day warranted a change in schedule, the better to lend moral support to my father, a soldier riding into battle while carrying the banner high for the entire neighborhood.

To truly appreciate the importance of the occasion, you would have had to follow along with my father as he left our house and proceeded down Herbert Street to Sill School, approximately four blocks away. More important than the physical distance was the dramatic change in the houses and their occupants along the way. As Father walked farther west, the houses and lots became larger and the number of shade trees increased from two to three per block to a one-per-house ratio. After the first block, all of the occupants seated on the porches and draping the steps were White. They were not to be confused with the Polish, Hungarian, and Jewish families of our area who were white, but not White.

Surprisingly, although few of the White families knew my father by name, they all knew him by reputation. As he walked past their houses, they either nodded their head in greeting or muttered good morning. My father solemnly returned their greeting in kind. Not until he had passed from view did you begin to hear their screen doors slam shut. As the doors closed in descending order, the sound created a peculiar rhythm of its own.

Obviously forewarned, Mrs. Pringle, the vice principal, was waiting with me for my father at the front door of the school. She immediately said, "I'm afraid there's been a misunderstanding, but I'm sure we can resolve it quickly."

"I certainly hope so," my father responded. "I would hate to take a day off from work and not get the matter cleared up."

We went directly to the home economics classroom to talk to the new teacher, Miss Clark. She was a rather nondescript looking young woman with limp blonde hair and faded blue eyes, probably all of twenty-two years of age. When introduced to my father, she nervously explained, "There's obviously been a misunderstanding. I would never do anything to hurt any of the children."

As the meeting got underway, I went to my assigned seat, sat down, and attempted to blend into the woodwork. The adults seemed to forget I was there, so I was able to see and hear the entire meeting. My father began by describing how upset my mother was about the situation. "Of course," he said, "anything that upsets my wife upsets me." Then he leaned back and waited for a response.

During the ensuing silence, Miss Clark nervously chewed her bottom lip while Mrs. Pringle idly doodled on the notepad before her. As the silence deepened, first Miss Clark and then Mrs. Pringle struggled to say something, but the words died before they were fully formed. Finally, my father broke the prolonged silence.

Staring directly into Mrs. Pringle's eyes, he said, "When you really give the situation some thought, there is a simple solution to the problem. Just rotate the window washing and floor mopping assignment through all the home economics students. It's the only fair way to handle the situation."

Neither Mrs. Pringle nor Miss Clark had any way to know what a large concession this proposal represented for my father. It was well known in our family that Father considered floor mopping and window washing as very detrimental to a female's health. A doctor friend of his had once told him that if all women would refrain from performing these two chores, the number of deaths from premature births and miscarriages would drop, dramatically. The one time I knew Father to completely lose his temper with my brother was the day he found my mother mopping the kitchen floor while William read a science fiction magazine in the bedroom. It never happened again!

Though unaware of this background, both the vice principal and Miss Clark agreed that this was the perfect solution to the problem, and the meeting was adjourned.

Back in the neighborhood, there was both excitement and satisfaction at my father's handling of the situation. Of course there were as many versions of the incident as there were home economics students. In succeeding days, the story was amplified and embellished at every telling. By the end of the week, the latest version contained not only a description of the actual meeting but also included the relating of an alleged conversation between my father, Mrs. Pringle, and Miss Clark. In this conversation, my father had demanded Miss Clark's resignation but eventually withdrew his request after copious tears from both the vice principal and Miss Clark. Since I was the only student who had actually been in the room during the meeting, my confirmation of the various versions was eagerly sought. I am ashamed to confess that I confirmed or denied their legitimacy based solely on how well I liked, or disliked, the author.

In the days that followed, Mr. Kraus, owner of Kraus's Shoe Repair, offered to resole our shoes free of charge. Micah, the Hungarian clerk at the local A&P store, was observed deliberately cracking the ends of perfectly whole eggs in order to sell them to my mother at two for a penny. Mrs. Allen gave my mother two matching fabric flour sacks. The material in these sacks was highly prized for making school dresses. As Mrs. Allen had two preteen daughters, this gift, more than any other, really touched my mother's heart.

The gifts were our neighbors' way of saying thank you to my father for giving them an enhanced sense of self worth. My father understood, and although he hated charity worse than God hated sin, he accepted the gifts graciously.

Gradually, the atmosphere at school returned to normal, and interest in the home economics affair faded. It was soon replaced by the next neighborhood crisis. The frown on Mrs. Pringle's face was replaced by a tentative smile. Then, copies of the new assignment list for the home economics class were distributed, and all hell broke loose.

At first, little attention was paid to the new schedule, but as more and more "little darlings" arrived home with red, chapped hands from the harsh chemicals used to clean the windows and floors, more and more irate white parents appeared in the school office to complain vigorously.

Mrs. Pringle appeared at her wit's end. Needless to say, I kept Father fully informed of all developments. As I related the day's events, he and Uncle Smitty would sit with creased brows, intently analyzing the data in an attempt to develop defense strategies against the attack that would surely come. No chess master assessing the next move of his opponent deliberated more carefully than my father and uncle as they developed defenses against possible negative moves that the system might make. The longer it took the system to act, the more anxious they became. Finally, the suspense ended.

It was on a late fall afternoon in October that I was called into Mrs. Pringle's office and given a long, sealed envelope to deliver to my father. She cautioned me not to stop, anywhere, on the way home. The content of the envelope was very important, and she wanted my father to get it as soon as possible. For the first time in memory, I did not wait on Beatrice. Instead, grasping the envelope tightly in my hand, I raced home. Gasping for breath, I lunged up the back steps and into the kitchen, thrusting the now damp envelope into my mother's hand.

My mother looked at the face of the envelope, then held it loosely in her left hand as if she did not quite know what to do with it. Finally, she walked into the living room and placed it on the half-moon-shaped end table by the front door. Without uttering a word, my mother took my hand and led me to the daybed, where we both sat down. In complete silence, we patiently awaited my father's return from work.

Fortunately, or unfortunately, depending upon your viewpoint, my father was working overtime. It was the beginning of the fall social season, and the kitchen staff at the Detroit Sheraton Hotel was working overtime in an attempt to keep up with the hotel's calendar of events. It was after 7:00 P.M. before we heard the sound of Father's footsteps on the back steps. He stopped at the kitchen sink to wash his hands, then entered the living room and sat down in his rocking chair. As usual, he looked at my mother and said, "How's everything going, Gracie—what's for dinner?"

Impatiently, I ran to get Father his newspaper, placing the envelope on top. He looked at the envelope, turning it over and over in his hands, before opening it. At last, he broke the seal, took out the one page letter, and proceeded to read and reread it several times.

Both my mother and I held our breath in anticipation of his reaction. With each rereading, the furrows in his forehead deepened. Finally, he looked up from the letter and said, "Listen to this, Gracie. 'It has come to the attention of this office that there exists a board of education labor management agreement that forbids performance of school maintenance work by anyone other than union maintenance workers. In order to conform to the requirements of this agreement, the teaching of housekeeping chores has been dropped from the home economics curriculum.' "

The letter was signed by the vice principal and countersigned by a Mr. William Marshall Jr., president of the Detroit Board of Education.

By the time Father finished reading the letter out loud, he was choked with laughter. After he caught his breath, he said, "I knew that 'The Man' would find a way out. He owes me a cigar. Baby, go tell Uncle Smitty to come here right away. I can't wait to see his face when he reads this!"

As I raced down the back steps and out the back gate, I heard my father burst into a new wave of laughter. I could still hear him laughing as I turned the corner and headed down Scotten Avenue toward my uncle's house.

DICK TRACY'S NOT YOUR FRIEND

Everyone in our neighborhood knew that naming a boy Ronnie was definitely asking for trouble. In fact no self-respecting male in the entire area would allow himself to be addressed by any name ending in *ie*. Ronnie Harmon, however, was mentally retarded, and his name fit him just fine. Many retarded children were called dim-witted, slow, or even crazy, but Ronnie was always referred to by his given name.

The Harmon family lived on the first floor of an apartment building directly across the street from our house. The mother was a short, slim, fair-complexioned woman who always wore a hat and gloves. Winter or summer, early or late, if you saw Mrs. Harmon, she wore a hat and carried gloves. Mr. Harmon was a male version of his wife with a snap-brim hat and tie replacing her hat and gloves. My father said, "Mr. and Mrs. Harmon put the lie to the old maxim that only opposites attract."

Although he never said so, I believe my father secretly admired Mr. Harmon. They were physically alike, and newcomers to the neighborhood often asked if Mr. Harmon and my father were brothers. They were both meticulous dressers and shared an obsession, bordering on mania, for tailor-made suits. My father had married late in life. In prior years he had been responsible only for himself and was accustomed to wearing the finest clothes. The birth of his children put a damper on this custom, although he did manage to secure an occasional new suit by trading his carpentry skills for those of a tailor on Milford Avenue.

It was his respect and admiration for Mr. Harmon that made what followed so devastating for my father. Three days before Christmas, Mr. Harmon went out for a pack of cigarettes and never returned.

It was my father who first noticed his absence. Mr. Harmon worked as a waiter at the Detroit City Club, and my father worked at the Sheraton Hotel, as a

cook. Each workday, they would meet at a downtown bus stop for the long ride home. Monday through Friday, they would turn the corner of Bangor and Herbert at about 6:15 P.M. Waiting on the front porch, we would run to meet our father while Ronnie banged on his front window in recognition of his father's arrival. Mr. Harmon never waved back, which seemed to puzzle my father. "Oh, well," he told my mother. "perhaps he's just tired."

My mother did not respond but continued putting supper on the table.

Although it was my father who first noticed Mr. Harmon's absence, it was my mother who finally garnered enough courage to approach Mrs. Harmon. One day, she baked several loaves of apple butter bread, Ronnie's favorite, wrapped one in waxed paper, and went across the street to visit. It was several hours before she returned.

Upon entering the house, she did an unusual thing. Instead of proceeding to the kitchen, which was her customary haven, she plopped down on the daybed in the living room and rested her head on the back cushion. Both my brother and I gasped in amazement. No one, except Father, ever sat on the daybed. Although it was a full-sized sofa that could open to form a double bed, we seldom used it unless we had an overnight guest. It was only in moments of high emotional distress that it served as a safe harbor for family members.

There, my mother sat as if she sat there everyday. An overwhelming silence filled the room to overflowing, but no one spoke. My father seemed to realize that my mother would speak when she was ready, and not a moment before.

Mother raised her head and looked at us long and hard. Finally, she nodded her head as if in answer to some unspoken question. Turning to my father, but including us in her surveillance, she said, "William, I really don't know what the world is coming to. Alvin Harmon left his family because he couldn't accept having a mentally handicapped son. Doesn't he understand that handicapped or not he's still his son? That it's because of his handicap that he needs him so much?"

Father stared off into space for a while before replying, "Gracie, you're always saying that only God can judge the heart. Maybe we had better leave the judging to him. It's Mamie Harmon who needs our help now."

Suddenly, the tension left my mother's body like air escaping from a balloon. She looked at my father with a firm expression and said, "You're right. William, I'll just have to live by my own rules."

My brother and I also sat in silence but for an entirely different reason. We were in a state of shock as we realized that, for the first time in our young lives, our mother and father had discussed a problem concerning adults in our presence without reservation. No shooing us out of the room. No talking in code. No retiring to their bedroom to discuss the matter as we listened at the door hearing only enough to completely confuse us. It was clear that our parents had decided that we were old enough to hear and understand the everyday tragedies of life. Never again was anything hidden from us. How proud we were to be considered mature enough to face life head on. We did not realize that our parents, after much argument and deliberation, had decided they could no longer let us believe in a world that was all peaches and cream. Reality had to play its part. This change was none too soon. In a few months, reality would seize us all in its iron grip and refuse to let go.

The neighborhood rallied around Ronnie and his mother. At first, Ronnie would bang on the window when he saw my father return in the evening while crying out something that sounded faintly like "Da! Da!" As the months went by, he stood at the window less and less often.

When the elderly woman who lived in the apartment above the Harmons lost her job, she offered to move in with Mrs. Harmon and care for Ronnie during the day for room and board. Sister Young was too old for the job, but between daily drop-in visits from my mother, Mrs. Eubanks, and Aunt Bessie, she managed well enough.

Of course the Church of the True Believers took full credit for the resolution of Mrs. Harmon's baby-sitting problem. Whenever a member of the church took part in any activity that could be remotely considered Christian in nature, the church took credit for it. This grandstanding infuriated my father to no end because the Harmon's name was added to the church's prayer list only at the insistence of my mother.

On my tenth birthday, Uncle Smitty took me shopping. He said I could get two presents, as long as they were not too expensive. Oh, what a delicious dilemma! The possibilities were endless. Mother mentioned such items as new shoes, socks, even petticoats and panties, but my uncle insisted that I, alone, make the decision. I finally decided on a red purse from Ruben's Department Store and a pink, silk-covered diary from Kresge's Five-and-Dime. The purse contained a small mirror, and the diary had its own key, the better to protect my secrets. As we loitered in the toy department of the five-and-dime, my uncle spied a small toy pistol with a leather handle. We both said his name at the same time, "Ronnie."

Everyone knew that Ronnie loved toy guns. The mere sight of one would send him into gales of laughter as he struggled fiercely to gain possession. Every time Mrs. Harmon saw this reaction, she would promise to get him one next week.

With her limited funds, next week never came. When my uncle bought the gun for Ronnie, I was as pleased as punch. From the day he received it, Ronnie was never seen without his gun. His mother said he even slept with it.

One day, the captain from the local police precinct came through the neighborhood. Most of the police in the area were white and greatly feared, but the captain was different. It wasn't that he loved Negroes, he just loved people. He and my father seemed to have something in common because he always stopped at our house for a few minutes. Many years later, I learned they had known each other at another time and place. In fact, in their teens, they rode the rails together. My uncle claimed that was the reason the police went easy on our neighborhood.

Despite city regulations that required each patrolman to spend a specific number of hours in each area, the police department ran very few patrols in our neighborhood. The captain got around the rule by taking two days out of each month and flooding the neighborhood with all available staff. Our streets would be filled with groups of veteran patrolmen accompanied by young rookies just beginning to learn the ropes. The captain would take advantage of this period to chat with tradespeople and visit with my father. Our neighbors did not resent their relationship, since a word to my father had gotten more than one of their sons out of trouble.

I shall never forget the scene on that Saturday morning. One of the senior officers—whose name I've since forgotten—was standing on the curb in front of Mrs. Harmon's apartment building talking with Reverend Elder. In predominantly Negro neighborhoods, the law and the church always tried to stay on good terms. They both benefited from a harmonious relationship. My father and the captain were standing at the corner, looking back down the street, when, suddenly, Mrs. Harmon came out of the front door of the apartment building followed by Ronnie, who was waving his toy pistol and screaming, "Bang! Bang!" The officer's and Reverend Elder's backs were to the apartment building, and they did not see the rookie cop whirl and pull the gun from his holster. My brother looked up, then screamed, "No!" Almost simultaneously, the captain and my father looked that way. Although I could not hear what they said, I will never forget their contorted faces. Their mouths took on the shape of those hideous gargoyles pictured atop ancient buildings in Europe.

The senior officer turned, but it was too late. The sound of three bullets filled the air. It was the loudest sound I had ever heard. The bullets hit with such force that they lifted Ronnie's slight body completely off the ground. When the sound died down, he lay spread eagle on the sidewalk like a puppet that had lost his puppeteer. All that remained was the sound of his mother's screams.

The captain asked if he could speak at the funeral. He wanted to offer his regrets and condolences, to tell the neighborhood that the young rookie was heartbroken and on the verge of a nervous breakdown. It was his first day on the street, and perhaps the department had made a mistake. Perhaps the force had pushed him too hard. He wanted to say that it was all a horrible mistake that the police department would do anything to undo.

Reverend Elder turned down his request. She said the wound was too raw, and the anger too deep. To avoid any trouble, she barred all police officers from the funeral service.

The police officers were not the only ones absent from the funeral. Mrs. Harmon was unable to locate Ronnie's father, and he did not learn of his son's death until over five years later.

The captain asked my father to accompany him to Mrs. Harmon's apartment. He thought she would not refuse to see him if my father was there. Although she opened the apartment door, Mrs. Harmon refused to accept the money the department had collected. Father knew she wanted to return Ronnie's body to Alabama for burial. He persuaded her to accept the collection. Still offering profuse apologies and condolences, the captain left the building and headed for his car.

As he opened his car door, the captain waved goodbye to Reverend Elder, who was climbing the church steps. Pointing to several children who stood nearby singing and clapping their hands, he said, "Well, Reverend, at least the children don't hate us."

The Reverend stopped on her way up the steps and answered, "I think you had better listen carefully to what they're singing."

The captain's face blanched as he listened to the words of the song sung to the tune of "The Farmer in the Dell."

"Dick Tracy's not your friend! Dick Tracy's not your friend! Hi Ho the Merrio. Dick Tracy's not your friend."

Uncle Smitty left town the day after Ronnie died. Although no one blamed him for what had happened, he blamed himself. The evening of that fateful day, he sat in our kitchen, with his head cupped in his hands, mumbling over and over again, "Bill, why did I buy him that damn toy gun? Why?"

My father could only respond, "It's not your fault. It was an accident. Anyone could have brought him that gun."

All efforts to console Uncle Smitty failed. Sometime during the night, he left town.

For the next few days, it was uncharacteristically quiet at our house. Friday afternoon, a telephone message was left at Roosevelt Drug Store for my father. A Miss Freddie Williams reported that Uncle Smitty was all right and staying in Chicago with her. This was our family's introduction to my uncle's latest romantic fling, but it was not to be our last. Throughout the rest of that year, the occasional letter arrived from Chicago, written first by Miss Freddie and finally by my uncle. A year later, he turned up at our house, none the worse for wear.

An uneasy truce developed between the neighborhood and the police. It ended almost a year later when an officer was injured rescuing two little girls from a burning house on Bangor Street. They had been left alone while their parents attended a prayer meeting. Suddenly, the singing of the Dick Tracy rhyme was forbidden, and our parents again exchanged pleasantries with the occasional patrolman who walked our streets. When the injured officer miraculously recovered from his burns, the Church of the True Believers immediately claimed full credit, as the injured children's father, notorious for his long-winded prayers, was chairman of the deacon board.

THE MEMORIAL

The months following Ronnie's death seemed to move in slow motion. Although the Harmons were seldom mentioned by name, statements such as "Wasn't that the saddest thing you've ever seen?" and "You'd think a grown man would know the difference between a toy gun and a real revolver!" brought them instantly to mind. The neighborhood had experienced many tragedies, but this one proved particularly difficult to accept. Gradually, all public discussions ended, although you would often see people who were passing the spot where Ronnie had spilled his life's blood stop to silently pay their respects.

If Ronnie's death proved difficult for adults to handle, it left the neighborhood children awash in a sea of grief and fear. It was the way he died, more than the death itself, that left us unable to sleep at night and struggling to swallow the lump that seemed to hang permanently in our throats. We knew it could have been any one of us. His death contained the essence of every sermon and Sunday school lesson we had ever heard. For the warning "No man knows the hour of the day that the Son of God cometh!" was the common thread running through all sermons and lessons. Soaked in sin and ill prepared to meet our maker, fear ran rampant through our ranks. To the untrained eye, we appeared as happy and carefree as always, but underneath was a deep uneasiness that caused us to watch each other with wary eyes.

It was my father who first noticed our distress. Although he had never set foot in the Church of the True Believers, one evening after supper he waited on the church steps for Reverend Elder to arrive for the Wednesday night prayer meeting. Ever on the alert for a chance to be with him, I tagged along.

Although Reverend Elder seemed surprised to see my father, she greeted him with a smile. When he declined her invitation to enter the church, she asked if there was anything she could do for him. He replied, "No, but there is something the church can do for the neighborhood. Our children need help, and it's up to us to provide it."

Upon hearing my father's words, Reverend Elder appeared to relax. Exhaling a deep sigh, she said, "Then there is something wrong! It's not just my imagination! Ronnie's death has really upset the whole neighborhood, but it's the children that I worry about. I wish there was something we could do to help them."

At this point, Father lowered his voice. I could barely hear what they were saying. It seemed he was suggesting that perhaps the church could sponsor a project for the children to take their minds off the tragedy. Maybe stage a concert or a play. That way, all the children could be included.

I shook my head in disbelief. Surely I had heard wrong! The Church of the True Believers stood firmly against movies and the theater. Both were considered the work of the Devil. Because he allowed us to attend the Saturday matinees at the Rogers Theater, Father was seen as a prime example of how easily the Devil could weave his wicked web. Because of my mother's standing in the church, they were afraid to openly attack him, but they did throw an occasional scornful glance his way.

The Reverend stood lost in thought. Finally, with a deep sigh, she looked at my father and said, "All right, Mr. Sprague, we'll work something out."

Thus was born that magnificent theatrical epic entitled "Beloved of God."

When Father told Mother about the project, she gasped in amazement and asked, "However will the Reverend sell the idea to the congregation? Why, the deacon board will have a fit. They even objected to members going to see the movie *Green Pastures*, and Lord knows that's about as spiritual as you can get."

Father replied, "I don't know, Gracie, but I think your Reverend is a lot smarter than we give her credit for. I think she'll hold her own against the deacons and then some."

Father's assessment proved right. Following the Sunday morning service, Reverend Elder announced the formation of the Sunday School Players, which would consist of all the neighborhood children interested in joining. As a murmur of dissent moved through the congregation, she hastened to add that the purpose of the group would be to write and perform a play as a memorial to Ronnie Harmon. It would be an excellent opportunity for the church to teach the neighborhood children about the goodness of the Lord. Leaning forward in the pulpit, she said, "Who knows, perhaps souls will be saved."

When my mother describe the scene to my father, he laughed and said, "I told you she was clever. She really put the deacons between a rock and a hard place. They might be able to argue against a memorial for Ronnie but not against the possibility of saving souls."

Grudgingly, they conceded defeat.

When news of the project reached our level, absolute chaos broke out. By four o'clock Monday afternoon, kids from all over the neighborhood had converged on the grassy knoll behind Lothrop Library. The group was so large that the head librarian came out to see what was going on. When she finally understood the situation, she offered to help us write the play. Since my brother and I attended more Saturday movie matinees that anyone in the neighborhood, we were named head writers. There followed a frenzy of mental activity, which, had they known of it, would have gladdened the hearts of our teachers at Sill School.

The fact that it took us a week to write the play gives some indication of the importance we attached to the project. Pencils were worn down to the nub. We literally ran out of erasers as we wrote and rewrote the lines of the epic. In fact, we worked so hard that we worked ourselves out of our grief and fear. To be honest, I don't think any of us thought about Ronnie other than as a character in our play.

When the script was completed, one problem remained. How would we find roles for all of the children who had signed up to take part in the play? My father said to leave everything to him. He had an idea that might solve the problem. Less than one month later, after numerous rehearsals, the production was ready. Excitement had reached fever pitch. Even the initial dissenters anxiously awaited opening night. At 7:00 P.M., on the first Saturday in August, the curtain rose on the Sunday School Players' first production, "Beloved of God."

In the end, the title was the head librarian's sole contribution to the play. When she mentioned that the Navaho Indians had a word they used to describe all handicapped persons as "Beloved of God," we had our title. The play, itself, resulted from the efforts of a small group within the Sunday School Players, with imaginations as big as all outdoors, combined with the gentle influence of Reverend Elder and my father. It was not until years later that I realized how skillfully the Reverend and my father had led the congregational sheep to the slaughter and changed the direction of the Church of the True Believers forever.

Although the church deacons had warmed to the memorial project, they balked when we asked permission to temporarily remove the lectern from the pulpit in order to create one large stage. While Mother and Aunt Bessie were debating how best to convince the deacons that it would not be a sacrilege to temporary move the lectern, Mrs. Eubanks asked, "Why not split the stage? Have two stages instead of one."

From the mouth of a woman who had never been inside a picture show or a theater came the perfect solution. Since the play had two acts, which represented different times and locations; we hung separate curtains on each side of the lectern. The first act took place on the left stage, and the second act on the right. The play must go on, and it did.

The audience sat in rapt attention as the curtain lifted to show Ronnie (Kenneth English) and Mrs. Harmon (Marvin Sprague) seated on chairs in the center of a living room. The furnishings had been borrowed from all over the neighborhood. If you looked closely, you could see little tags attached to each item with the owner's name on it. Even the writer, who lived in the little house on the alley, had volunteered a lamp and a chair. There were appreciative comments from the audience. Murmurs of "Doesn't it look real," to "You know, he does look a lot like Ronnie," circled the room.

Approval grew as it was noted that Mrs. Harmon was reading to Ronnie from the Bible. Such passages as "Suffer the little children and forbid them not, to come unto me: for such is the kingdom of heaven," and "Thou shall love the Lord thy God with all thy heart, and with all thy soul, and with all thy mind," brought forth a chorus of Hallelujahs! Amen's! and Praise the Lord!

By the time she had reached the Ten Commandments, many of the saints were on their feet, clapping hands and shouting praises to the heavens. My father said, "Anybody passing by on the street would have sworn they were holding a revival inside."

As the first act moved toward its climax, the audience became quiet. The problem of how to show Ronnie's death had proved so difficult that we had sought help from my father and the Reverend. The result was a scene that showed Ronnie looking out of the living room window, while in the background I described the events leading up to his death. There wasn't a dry eye in the house. The dainty white handkerchiefs of the women and the vibrantly colored kerchiefs of the men blended together like a field of wildflowers blown gently by the stifled sighs and tears of the audience. At the moment of the shooting, represented by the beat of a hammer on a garbage can lid, many of the ladies in the audience broke into tears. When the curtain came down, there was a moment of silence and then thunderous applause. During the intermission, there was much milling about. Every family in the audience had at least one child participating in the play, and congratulations rang throughout the room. By the end of the intermission, the audience had settled into their seats, anxious to see what the second act would bring.

When the curtain rose, the audience gave a collective gasp of delight. The stage was covered with crepe paper flowers and vines. A huge basket of artificial flowers, borrowed from the window of Reuben's Department Store, held center stage. Framed pictures adorned the sidewalls of the stage, and figurines, glass vases, and decorative bowls sat on several small tables. My mother had donated the use of several crocheted tablecloths, which were draped over my father's workbench. Everyone who had anything they cherished as beautiful had donated it for display. The church secretary had made large crepe paper bluebirds that hung from the ceiling and swayed slightly from the motion of the actors on stage. But it was the quilt mounted against the back wall that drew everyone's attention. It was my sister Jewel's crazy quilt, which had not been seen since her death.

The months following Jewel's death had been hard on the family. Although we seldom spoke of Jewel, it was obvious that she was on everyone's mind. Gradually, we began to speak openly about how much we missed her and of the hole her death had left in the family. Although the sense of loss would remain for a lifetime, the public display of Jewel's quilt signaled the beginning of a return to normalcy.

The scene opened with Ronnie seated on the floor with his back to the audience. He appeared weak and listless. As he unfolded his legs and stood erect, the audience saw that he had completely changed from the pale, listless, creature of the first act. He was dressed in white, and his legs and arms were straight and strong. Gradually, from all corners and sides of the stage, figures began to appear. Angels, numberless angels, filled the stage. The angels were my father's solution to the problem of how to accommodate all the would-be actors on stage. They came from all directions, and as each passed Ronnie, they seized his hand, twirled him in a circle, and then moved off to make room for the next angel. Dressed in their mother's best white sheets, which had been bleached almost to the point of extinction, they flitted back and forth as their silver cardboard wings glistened in the bright lights. The message was clear. Tears rolled down Mrs. Eubanks cheeks as she murmured over and over, "He's bound for Glory! He's bound for Glory!"

On each side of the rear stage, a platform was placed, consisting of three shallow steps. After each angel had their moment in the spotlight, they would turn, move toward one of the platforms, and climb the steps with arms outstretched. When they reached the top, they would be lifted off by one of the men standing behind the curtain as though they were on their way back to the "throne of grace."

The exit of each angel brought down the house. By the time the last two angels had escorted Ronnie up the steps into my father's waiting arms, the audience had exhausted itself both physically and emotionally.

When order returned, Reverend Elder was wise enough to simply give the benediction and wish everyone a safe journey home. The audience left still rehashing the high points of the evening.

Reverend Elder went backstage to thank my father for his help. It was the first time I had seen him shake a woman's hand. Without knowing how I knew, I recognized that handshake as a high honor. From the look on the Reverend's face, so did she.

The memorial for Ronnie cast a warm glow over the neighborhood. It provided an emotional release and began the healing process. There was talk of a repeat performance, but Reverend Elder nipped that idea in the bud.

The following Sunday, she explained that a true memorial service was a one-time affair, designed to honor the person's life and not to merely entertain. She did mention the possibility of other projects for the Sunday School Players, such as Easter, Mother's Day, and Christmas programs. The response to this suggestion did not come until the next Sunday when nine of the children who had participated in the play marched down the center aisle and gave their lives to the Lord.

The Christmas pageant drew a full house. Plans were immediately made for the Easter program. The Sunday School Players expanded to include many adults. The programs became so popular that members fought to participate, and Reverend Elder resorted to a rotational system. Each time my mother mentioned another church program, my father would smile and give her a wink. Struggling to hide a smile, she would respond, "All right, Mr. Sprague. All right."

But the deacons had the last word. They never did give permission for that lectern to be moved.

NOT BY BREAD ALONE

After Ronnie Harmon's death, Father became obsessed with the idea that his children needed greater exposure to things cultural. We had always attended church concerts and listened to the Saturday afternoon broadcasts from the Metropolitan Opera House in New York, during opera season. Thanks to the generosity of Uncle Smitty, we often attended the Sunday concerts held at the band shell on Belle Isle in the summer. During my grade school years, the Detroit Public School System prided itself on providing wide ranging cultural experiences for the little "urchins" living in the less prosperous areas of Detroit. Sill School students were bombarded by a series of trips to automobile plants, local radio stations, as well as an annual dip into the thrills of the Ringling Brothers, Barnum and Bailey Circus. Visiting ballet companies sent fledging dance apprentices to perform at the school. While the boys squirmed in embarrassment, the girls sat wrapped in delight, imagining themselves up on the stage twisting and twirling in the arms of the male dancers. In spite of all of this, Father still appeared depressed whenever he spoke of feeding the spirit as well as the mind and body.

It was while waiting with the other chauffeurs in an anteroom of the Masonic Temple that my father heard his first opera. It was love at first sound. He was convinced that if his children were exposed, they, too, would develop a love for opera.

During the opera season, whatever my brother and I were doing at two o'clock on a Saturday afternoon had to be shut down so that we could sit around the radio and listen to the opera while Father described the storyline. The first broadcasts were exciting. We felt very grown up, for our father was introducing us to a world he had sometimes described but never shared. As the opera season went on and on, we became bored and restless. Although Father tried his best to describe what he knew was happening on the stage in New York, it lost something in the translation. In frustration, he said, "Gracie! They need to see and hear it live. I can't describe the scenery, the costumes, the acting, and the excitement of a live performance!"

Mother replied, "William, you're doing your best. That's all you can do," but she knew her reassurances fell on deaf ears.

It was more than a year later when Mr. Robinson told him about the job he had found with a cleaning service. Immediately, Father's ears perked up. It seemed the cleaning agency was looking for people willing to clean theaters in the evening. They had no problem finding people to clean offices, because the work could be completed within a four-hour time frame in the early evening. The theaters, however, were a different matter. The cleaning personnel could not begin work until the theater had emptied after the evening performance. They rarely finished their work before one or one thirty the next morning.

My father soon earned a reputation as a reliable employee. Theater managers began to ask for him by name. When he thought the time was right, he put his plan into action. He asked the manager of the Shubert Lafayette Theatre if he could bring his children to work with him one night. Perhaps they could sit in the empty seats at the rear of the auditorium. He promised we would be well behaved, and that he wouldn't even know we were there. At first, the manager was a little hesitant—he didn't know what the theater patrons might think—but since Bill was such a good worker, he finally said, "Okay, we'll give it a try."

When Father woke us at two o'clock in the morning, we wondered what all the excitement was about. He said something about going to see a stage play next Friday. We grunted "uh huh," and promptly fell back to sleep. In the light of day, we began to feel excited about the prospect of seeing a real, live play. Although Father had often tried to describe live theater to us, we would see it for ourselves. We felt very important. We did not know anyone, other than our father, who had seen a play on the legitimate stage.

Father laid out his battle plan, paying close attention to every minute detail. He had long sessions with my mother, who would play a major role in the success or failure of the enterprise. She smiled in amusement when he said, "Gracie, I want them to look special. This is a great opportunity. If Mr. Monroe accepts them being there this Friday, he may let me bring them down for other shows. Don't let me down."

Mother was a long time in responding. She seemed to be weighing her words before speaking. When she did speak, she said, "William, you know you're doing something you swore you'd never do. You're putting your children on exhibition for the entertainment of 'the other man.' I'm really surprised."

I had never seen my mother so set against anything as she was to our going to the theater. Then, she did something that was unheard of; she mentioned it to Uncle Smitty when he came by the next evening. It wasn't that she had never discussed a situation with my uncle outside of Father's earshot, but they were usually minor requests for his assistance in getting Father to modify some extreme mandate. Together, they had worked to change my father's mind on many occasions. But this time it was different. Never before had Mother expressed total disagreement with one of Father's projects. My uncle listened attentively as she voiced her concerns.

Choking back tears, she said, "Smitty, you know I'm always the one who tries to tone William down when he starts talking that racial stuff. That's why I can't understand why he wants to turn the children into a sideshow for some white people he doesn't even know. I can just see it now. William won't be sitting with the children. If the children are made fun of, he won't even know it. Besides, why introduce them to a world that they will never be able to take part in. You've got to do something. I'm at my wit's end!"

Uncle Smitty patted my mother on the shoulder and promised he would do what he could.

Even though Mother was vehemently opposed to our going, she continued to make preparations for the outing. She completed work on a red velvet dress she was making for me; she used the material from a velvet bathrobe she had bought at the Goodwill Store for a nickel. Trimmed with a white lace collar, it was the equal of any of the expensive children's frocks to be found at Hudson's Department Store. Black patent leather slippers, from the shoe bin at the Goodwill, completed the outfit. They were one size larger than I needed, and the toes were scrapped white, but a little newspaper padding and black shoe polish soon solved these problems.

It was not until Thursday evening that Uncle Smitty returned to relate the gist of his conversation with my father. Mother leaned forward, eagerly, as he said, "Gracie, I had that conversation with Bill. I'm afraid I got an entirely different picture of the situation. Yes, he knows that he might be exposing his children to ridicule. Yes, he's aware that they may never have a chance to visit that world again. But he said, 'Smitty, it's worth the risk for them to have just one theater experience. If we don't believe that the future will be better than the present, what's the point of everything we're trying to accomplish?' "

In the end, they were both proven right.

At first, we were considered an oddity. But that didn't last long. The lady patrons who stopped to talk to us during intermission soon directed their attention to the garments we wore. The questions came hard and fast. "Wherever did you get that gorgeous dress? Helen, isn't this adorable? What a lovely dress shirt he's wearing. See how perfectly the ruffles fall."

My father had rehearsed us in how to respond to these inquiries. My brother sat in stony silence, too bashful to speak. I quickly said, "My dress was made from a bathrobe, and my brother's shirt was made from one of my uncle's old dress shirts."

I don't know what my father would have thought if he had heard me, but he didn't. Instead, my outburst generated numerous inquiries on how my mother could be contacted. From that first theater visit alone, Mother secured several months' worth of seamstress work. Father teased my mother by saying, "You see, Gracie, sometimes you have to do the wrong thing for the right reason."

Mother just smiled and returned to counting her potential earnings from the deluge of orders. They meant that she could add a little more to the savings she had secretly earmarked for a down payment on a house of our own.

As for my father, his reward was in seeing the look of wonder on our faces as we stared, transfixed, at the stage. He did not have to worry about our behavior because we were too awestruck to make any noise. I cannot remember a single word of dialogue, but I can close my eyes and see that stage, with its beautiful sets and costumes, bathed in the soft glow of multiple floodlights. I even remember the name of the play, *Captain Seeger*. It was magic!

For more than a year, my bother and I attended performances at various theaters in downtown Detroit. We even attended several operas performed by the touring company of the Metropolitan Opera. For weeks after, I went around imitating the tenor's rendition of the aria "Vesta la Giubba" from *Pagliacce*, sobs and all. Father would look over at Mother and say, "You see, Gracie, that's why I took the risk."

Gradually, the number of theater trips diminished. The cleaning company began letting people go, and my father sought a more permanent job situation. Although the trips ended, the benefits continued. We had been exposed to a world we did not know existed. It was a world that was to propel us ever forward.

1300 BEAUBIEN

During the 1930s and 1940s, the Detroit Police Headquarters was identified solely by its address, 1300 Beaubien. A large, ornate building, it covered half a city block. The very mention of that address was enough to strike fear into the hearts of Negroes anywhere in the city. If Dick Tracy was not your friend, then the inhabitants of 1300 Beaubien were your worst enemy!

To compound that fear, Detroit Negroes had their own personal nemesis residing at 1300 Beaubien, Mr. Bill Chandler. A former train porter and shoeshine boy, he was as well liked and respected by the police department management as he was hated and feared by his fellow Negroes. My father once described him as the poorest excuse for a cop he had ever seen.

Against this backdrop, you can readily understand Mother's terror when she was told that Father had accepted an offer to serve as chief numbers runner for the officers and employees of the Detroit Police Department. It was a simple system. All precincts fed their numbers bets into headquarters, at 1300 Beaubien, and the chief numbers runner picked them up and carried them to the central clearinghouse.

The system was absolutely foolproof, but only if you did the right thing. The previous runner, a Mr. Martin, had made the mistake of trying to cheat the numbers house. The following day, his lifeless body was found in the alley behind police headquarters. When my mother heard this, she increased the pressure on my father not to get involved. She cried, she begged, she pleaded. She even resorted to one of the oldest ploys known to womankind, saying, "If you loved me, you wouldn't do this." All to no avail.

My father was desperate. The hotel business had dropped to its lowest level in years. If he found work as a kitchen helper two days a week, he was lucky. One

evening, I overheard him tell my uncle, "Smitty, I don't know what I'm going to do. Gracie doesn't understand. It's been bad before but never like this. If I see another package of welfare cheese or eat another welfare grapefruit, I think I'll throw up. Practically every family I know is living on welfare, permanently. If something doesn't happen soon, we'll be in the same boat."

I believe my father would have done just about anything to stay off welfare. He hated charity with a vengeance. Whenever some man in the neighborhood would desert his wife and children and leave them to fend for themselves, he would invariably lean back in his rocking chair and quote his favorite scripture, 1 Timothy 5.8, "But if any provide not for his own . . . he has denied his faith and is worse than an infidel."

My aunt always said that my father quoted that scripture because it was the only one he knew.

The war between my mother and father concerning the numbers running continued. He tried to placate her by saying, "I'm running numbers for the police department. I couldn't be safer in my mother's arms."

Even my mother had to laugh at the thought of my father being carried in his mother's arms while a roll of betting slips streamed from his diaper. Then, she summoned courage to mention what was really on her mind. In a trembling voice, she asked, "What about Bill Chandler? Everyone says he's a mean, vicious, jealous-hearted cop. Most people avoid him like the plague, and here you are setting up shop on his home ground."

Father just smiled a mysterious smile and said, "I don't think I need to worry about Mr. Bill. Smitty knows him from his railroad days. He told me not to worry."

William and I sat quietly in a corner as the conversation went back and forth. Never had we seen our mother so persistent. It was years later that I came to understand the strength fear could generate in a woman who stands in protection of her home. Finally, my father gave in. Sitting in his rocking chair one evening, attempting to listen to the radio over my mother's continual verbal assaults, he surrendered. He turned off the radio, stood up, and in a flat, unemotional voice said, "Mrs. Sprague, I promise you on a stack of Bibles ten feet high that I will never set foot into 1300 Beaubien to collect a numbers slip."

When Mother bragged to Uncle Smitty about the pledge she had forced my father to make, he just laughed and said, "Gracie, if Bill said he would not set foot in 1300 Beaubien to collect a numbers slip, you can bet he won't."

He was still laughing as he went out the door.

Days, weeks, and months passed with little change in the pattern of our daily lives. My father left a little earlier for work and returned a little later. No one thought anything of it, for the streetcar lines were forever changing their schedules. Things were looking up. Father found enough part-time cooking assignments to fill the week. The jobs even seemed to pay better. The family finances were improving, and my brother and I returned to our weekly visits to the Rogers Theater. There we could lose ourselves to a world where Tom Mix stood tall in the saddle as he consistently rescued the damsel in distress while laying waste the film's villain; where the Northwest Mounted Police did the same in eight-part serials, which ended each week in nail-biting suspense; where Mae West sashayed across the screen, inviting one and all to "come up and see me sometime."

The calm my mother referred to as the Quiet Time was suddenly shattered by a report that Officer Duncan had been shot in the alley behind the pawn shop at Thirtieth and Warren. The news moved through the neighborhood like a shock wave. Of all the police officers at McGraw Station, Sean Duncan was the most unlikely prospect to land in trouble. Officer Duncan, or Dunk Can, as his fellow officers affectionately called him, came from a long line of police officers. His father, and his grandfather before him, had served as members of the force. He was the last of six brothers to enter the police academy and graduate to serve the people of Detroit. His five older brothers all graduated with honors, but Dunk Can barely squeaked through. Although his service was limited to desk assignments, he was nonetheless carrying on the family tradition. His father had secured the commissioner's promise to keep him assigned to internal projects. That promise was the price old Mrs. Duncan exacted before she would allow Sean to follow in his brothers' footsteps. When he heard of the shooting, Father said, "What in the world was Officer Duncan doing on a street assignment?"

Reverend Elder visited the Duncan family to express the neighborhood's condolences. On the way home, she stopped at our house. "Sister Sprague," she said, "Mrs. Duncan is beside herself with grief. She took on so that Dr. Robinson gave her a sleeping draft. The sergeant asked the church to pray for his family. Can you imagine that—an Irish-Catholic asking for prayer from a sanctified church. I think we should open the church for a prayer vigil."

As always in times of trouble, the Church of the True Believers became the focal point of the neighborhood. People came not only to pray for Officer Duncan and his family but also for the Peoples family as well, because it was young Remus Peoples who had shot the officer. When Officer Duncan, who was filling in for a fellow officer whose wife was being operated on, cornered Remus coming out of the Red Cross Pawn Shop, jewelry spilling from his pockets, Remus had raised a gun and shot the officer four times at point-blank range. Those at the scene when the ambulance arrived reported that Remus kept screaming, "I didn't know it was Officer Duncan! I didn't know it was Officer Duncan!"

The medics worked, feverishly, to contain the blood streaming from the wounds in the officer's chest. As they lifted him into the ambulance for the drive to Receiving Hospital, one said, "It's a miracle he's still alive. I don't think he'll make it to the emergency room."

But make it he did. Twenty-four hours later, he was still clinging to life, if only by his fingertips. Three days later, he was breathing on his own but still in a deep coma.

My father was inconsolable. He went by Receiving Hospital every day on his way home from work. My mother became quite worried and asked my uncle to keep an eye on him. Uncle Smitty said, "Don't worry, Gracie. Bill just has a lot on his mind."

As usual, my uncle was right. That night, Father put down his paper, turned to face my mother, and said, "Gracie, I have a confession to make. I've been running numbers over at police headquarters for the past six months. Officer Duncan hit 681 last Friday, and I don't know what to do with his winnings. Do I give them to his father, or should I give them to his wife? Rumor has it that they're separated. I wish Officer Duncan would regain consciousness. I don't want to do the wrong thing."

A look of complete amazement crossed my mother's face. "Running numbers," she said. "William, you gave me your word that you would not run numbers for the police or anybody else. I can't believe you went back on your word!"

Father hung his head and mumbled, "I promised you I wouldn't set foot in police headquarters to pick up numbers, and I kept my word. The janitor, Willie Washington, hands me the betting slips out of the side door every morning."

When Mother spoke, she said, "Well, Mr. Sprague, you got yourself into this mess without my help, and I'm sure you'll get yourself out the same way."

Over the next few days, my father and uncle held many huddled conferences. Although I strained to hear the conversations, their voices were too low. Mother spent most of her free hours working on a quilt intended for my brother's bed. She kept her gaze trained on making the tiny, almost invisible, stitches that were one of the hallmarks of her quilting. She did not join in the conversations.

The following Sunday, Uncle Smitty came in and hustled Father out to the back porch. Silent as the sphinx, I slipped into the bathroom, locked the door, and put my ear to a crack in the wall that overlooked the steps they were standing on. I was in time to hear my uncle say, "Don't worry, Bill. I know the commissioner is pressuring you to give Officer Duncan's winnings to his father, but first let me put Bill Chandler on the case. He owes me a favor, big time! Just let me handle this."

The next day, my father came home with a puzzled look on his face. Flopping down on the daybed, he said, "I know you're not speaking to me, Gracie, but the damnedest thing happened today. When I got to the side door of headquarters, instead of Willie, there was Bill Chandler with the betting slips in an envelope. You could have knocked me over with a feather! I don't know what Smitty has on him, but it must be a loo-loo! When I reached for the envelope, he began to speak faster than I have ever heard a man speak in my life. 'Look, Sprague,' he said, 'I've taken care of the commissioner. You just have to know how to handle him. I told him that you would do the same thing if the circumstances were reversed. If he had been shot after hitting the numbers, you would have held his winnings until you knew what he wanted you to do with them. He agreed that was the best thing to do. Tell Smitty we're even now.' "

Bill Chandler's statements were soon confirmed. When my father went to pick up the betting slips the next morning, he met the commissioner in the parking lot. The commissioner shook his hand and said, "Good man! Good man!"

The next Tuesday, Officer Duncan regained consciousness. After learning of his winning bet, the first words he uttered were, "Tell Bill to give half of my winnings to Lorraine and hold the other half until I see him."

Father did not hold his half for long. As soon as he got the message, he took off for Receiving Hospital. It was almost midnight when he reached the hospital, but the front desk let him up on the floor anyway. By this time, the story of Officer Duncan's lucky hit had circulate throughout the hospital. In all the excitement, Mother forgot that she was angry with Father, and tranquility returned to our house.

A few weeks later, Officer Duncan was released from the hospital. Of the four bullets he had taken, one remained in his body. It was located close to the spinal cord and considered inoperable. Eventually, he returned to work and was again assigned to a desk job at headquarters; however, this assignment was different. It was the assignment of an officer who had proved his valor in the line of duty and had earned the right to complete his career out of harm's way.

If my mother forgot her anger, my father did not forget her worry. On the day that Officer Duncan was released from the hospital, he turned the police headquarters numbers business over to Willie Washington. It was Willie who coined the expression, "If you want to make soup, you've got to put some beans in the pot."

Numbers players immediately seized upon this expression as justification for their illegal gambling. With my father's coaching, Willie soon became a shining light in the numbers business.

TOO MUCH OF A GOOD THING

It was Miss Pleasant who I first heard use the expression "Too much of a good thing."

Miss Pleasant wandered into the neighborhood when I was four years old and stayed to capture the heart of even the meanest person. Although some people made fun of her speech and dress, it would have cost a life if anyone hurt her. Dressed in the layered look, long before there was a layered look, she would wander from house to house doing small chores and thanking everyone "a hundred, million, trillion times" for the smallest kindness.

It was easy to find Miss Pleasant because every Monday her wash would be flapping on the clotheslines of whoever was hosting her that week. The pieces of her costumes, always black, were not identifiable as any specific fashion or style but, when assembled, were not unpleasant in appearance. She would stay a few weeks in one place, then suddenly pick up and move on. There was never a shortage of shelter or seats at the dinner table for Miss Pleasant. Father said that Miss Pleasant did more for the neighborhood than anyone he knew. Always smiling, always happy to see everyone, she would tilt her head to one side and say, "Hi sweetheart, you sure are good for the sore eyes," to male and female alike.

My curious mind struggled to understand what too much of a good thing could mean—if something was good, how could you have too much of it? Finally, I gave in and asked my mother for an explanation. While she made a valiant attempt to convey the meaning, I still didn't understand. Finally, I put it down as just another of Miss Pleasant's oddball expressions. Less than a year later, experience would teach me how wrong I was.

Every November, Grandma Alice mailed us a Thanksgiving box. The contents, which never varied, consisted of four five-pound cloth bags of her special pork sausage, three to four dressed roasting chickens packed in dry ice, a large bag of black walnuts from the walnut trees on the farm, apples and oranges, a container of mincemeat, a five-pound bag of hard candies, and several lengths of dress material. Since my mother shared the contents of the box with a few close friends, we were not the only ones who eagerly awaited its arrival. The arrival of the box was almost as good as Christmas.

Shortly before Thanksgiving Day, 1940, the box arrived. It was split on one side and re-taped on top, a battered but welcome sight. The postal service driver left it at the bottom of our steps after calling up the stairwell, "Package for the Sprague family."

Down the steps my brother and I rushed. I was twelve years old, and William was an old man of sixteen. We were finally old enough to be left on our own. On that Saturday, my father was at work, and my mother had gone to Canada with Aunt Bessie. It fell to us to rescue the magic box. We tugged and pushed the box up the steps until it lay safely at the front door of our flat. In a fever of excitement, we examined the package. It would be hours before our parents returned home. How could we survive the anxiety? What if something inside the battered box had spoiled? Wasn't it our duty to check out the contents? Normally, we wouldn't think of opening a package addressed to our parents, but this was an emergency. With a justifiably solemn expression on his face, my brother ripped open the top of the box. Turning it on its side, he dumped the contents onto the porch.

Grandma Alice had not failed us. Out tumbled the usual assortment of goodies. Nothing seemed to be missing. But wait! One of the cloth bags of sausage had opened, and the sausage had oozed out, spreading grease over the edge of one of the lengths of dress material. Perhaps we should cook some of the sausage to see if it was still good. Surely, when we explained the situation to Mama, she would understand.

In minutes, we had a skillet filled with sausage patties cooking on the back burner. Soon, an array of our friends ringed the bottom of the steps as the aroma of frying sausage wafted through the air. Drunk with power, we decided to cook another pan of sausage and share it with our friends.

It was only after we had cooked and eaten the second pan of sausage that we realized that the open bag of sausage was half empty. What could we say to our parents when they returned home? It was my brilliant brother who thought of a solution. "We've cooked so much of the bag already," he said, "we might as well cook the rest. Mama will just think that grandma sent three bags instead of four."

Having resolved the situation to our satisfaction, we cooked the balance of the bag of sausage. On into the afternoon we ate with ever decreasing pleasure. We sighed with relief as we finished the last of the sausage.

When Father returned from work, he found my brother asleep on the couch, while I was nodding in the rocking chair. He woke us up and asked, "Why are you kids so tired? Anyone would think you've been working all day. Your mother's not home yet? How about peanut butter sandwiches and tomato soup for supper?"

In a way, he was right. We had been working. Since late afternoon, we had worked at beating a path to the bathroom as the highly spiced sausage punished us for overeating.

We did not answer my father's question regarding supper but instead pointed to the box sitting on the kitchen table. Rubbing his eyes, my brother said, "That old box was heavy. Marvin and I had to drag it up all those steps. The tape was split, and stuff kept falling out all over everywhere. No wonder we're tired."

We held our breath as Father went to check on the box. Finally, he shook his head in disgust and said, "It doesn't make sense to deliver a package in this condition. Well, they won't get away with it. I'll stop off at the post office Monday and file a complaint."

Whew! Saved by the bell. The postal service could suffer our father's wrath far better than we could. One thing was certain, if I never saw another piece of sausage in my life, it would be too soon. Pleading extreme tiredness, my brother and I passed on supper and went straight to bed. As I lay in bed with the quilt pulled tightly around me, I thought to myself, All's well that ends well, and tucked the episode away in memory as a never-to-be-repeated experience.

While my brother and I were through with the episode, the episode was not through with us. What followed taught me that, contrary to popular belief, what you don't know could not only hurt you, it could kill you!

The following Monday, Father went to the post office to file the complaint. As he started out the front door, he turned and said, "Gracie, I'm going to take William with me. It's time he learned how to handle situations like this. If he doesn't learn soon, he'll spend the rest of his life letting people walk all over him."

My brother marched out the door behind Father with his head held high. He returned an hour later with this tail tucked between his legs. After what seemed like an eternity, he pulled me aside to break the bad news. In a tremulous whisper, he asked, "Why didn't you tell me that Grandma Alice always mailed a separate letter listing the contents of the box?"

"What are you talking about," I whispered back. "What letter?"

It seemed the letter was Grandma's way of insuring the safe arrival of the package. In case anything was lost or stolen, my parents could offer the letter as confirmation of the original contents of the package. The postal clerk, upon learning of the letter, told my father to bring it in when he received it, and the post office would conduct an investigation. Somewhere out there, among a million pieces of mail, was the epistle that would nail us to the cross. There was nothing we could do. Our fate lay in God's hands.

It is impossible to describe the misery we experienced in the next few days. We could neither eat nor sleep. Each day we rushed home from school to check the mail laying on the end table by the daybed. Each day we breathed a sigh of relief only to relapse into panic remembering that the doomsday letter was still out there, somewhere.

That Friday, we reached the end of our rope. We made an agreement that, if the letter did not arrive by Monday afternoon, we would confess, all, to our parents.

It was as if that agreement broke the logjam. When we returned home from school on Monday, the letter had arrived. There it lay on the end table, listing all the items that had been in the Thanksgiving package.

Mother called us into the kitchen and gave us oatmeal cookies and a glass of milk. Usually, this was our favorite treat, but not today. The hurt in my mother's eyes struck like a physical blow. Finally, she said, "Your father's working late tonight, but I don't want you to go to bed without seeing him. I think you know why. I'm too hurt to talk about it; he'll have to deal with you."

With that said, Mother withdrew to the comfort of her quilt scraps, and we withdrew to the misery of our guilt.

When Father arrived home that night, he found my brother and me sitting on the daybed, rigid with fear. Mother called him into the bedroom and closed the door. Silence descended over our house while we sat tensely awaiting the punishment we knew would come. Finally, the bedroom door opened, and we looked up to see Father towering over us. I closed my eyes, tightly, and clenched my fists until I drew blood. He bent down, and with a broad smile on his face, said, "Thanks for waiting up for me, but don't you think you should go to bed now. Tomorrow is a school day."

As Father continued down the hall toward the bathroom, Mother came out of the bedroom and leaned against the doorjamb looking down at us. I had seen that look on her face only once before, the day my father admitted that he had lied to her about running numbers. It was not until that moment that I realized how deeply our actions had hurt her. I looked at my brother, then broke into tears. William tried, valiantly, to hold back the tears, but one escaped and rolled down his cheek. As Mother dried my eyes with her handkerchief, she said, "I'm not going to punish you. I think you've been punished enough. Now I understand why you were so listless the day the box arrived. I want you to promise never to do anything like that again. Now go to bed and try to get some sleep."

Never was a promise more fervently given. Not only did I never do anything like that again, it was a very long time before I ate another piece of pork sausage. When I did, I found it strangely unappetizing. Or, as Miss Pleasant would say, "Too much of a good thing."

THE RED-AND-BLACK
CHINCHILLA COAT

Over the summer of 1940, I went from a don't-care tomboy to a fussy prima donna who would press and re-press a ruffle until it fell just so. To say that Mother was overjoyed at the change was the understatement of the year. In this new incarnation, happiness was a red-and-black wool chinchilla coat with gray fur collar and cuffs. That winter, my mother made me a very happy young lady. The story of the coat is as fascinating as the change that generated it.

Ever since I could remember, Mother's abilities as an expert seamstress were known far and wide. Mr. Campbell, who owned Campbell's Cleaners on McGraw Street, always said, "Miss Grace is far more than a seamstress; she's an artist."

In homage to her skills, he vowed to clean and press any of her creations free of charge.

My mother basked in the praise. Although normally the most modest of women, she was very vain concerning her dressmaking skills. When a disgruntled member of the Church of the True Believers dared to criticize her, Mrs. Eubanks soundly rebuked her by saying, "It's all right to be vain about your skills if you can back it up with deeds. I've never known Miss Grace to fail at anything she set her hand to, unlike some people I know."

It was this reputation that ultimately brought most of the female teachers at Sill School to our door. Beyond the normal repair and alteration work their garments required, my mother would often copy gowns from pictures in fashion magazines for them. Her work allowed them to have outfits in the height of fashion at a fraction of their original cost. In addition to the modest fees the teachers paid for the work, they would often give my mother bags of their outgrown and worn-out clothing. Father resented Mother accepting their castoffs, but he did not respond when Mother asked, "What's the difference in accepting their handouts for nothing and buying them at the Goodwill Store?"

When he saw how she used them, he never questioned her again.

On fall evenings, Mother would often pull out several bags of garments and sort them into two piles. One pile represented items that she thought she could do something with immediately. The other pile consisted of garments that might or might not be of use. When Mrs. Drummond gave her the ladies' red wool chinchilla coat, trimmed in gray fur, it went immediately into the second pile. The coat appeared thoroughly worn out. Even my mother could not disagree when my father said, "She ought to be ashamed to send you something in that condition. You'll just have to hold it for the garbage man. If it were me, I'd send it back to her!"

My mother just folded it neatly and added it to the stack of maybes.

Every evening, thereafter, my mother would pull out the coat and examine it closely. She examined the lining, the worn spots, and the fur trim over and over again. Every evening she would sigh, give it one more over all examination, and place it back in the maybe stack. Then one evening, she began to take the coat apart. My father looked on with interest because he knew this meant that she had discovered a use for the material. Even my brother appeared interested in guessing what that use might be. He applied his mathematical mind to the problem and came up with absolutely nothing.

The next afternoon, my mother took the segmented pieces of the coat to Mr. Campbell at Campbell's Cleaners. When he saw the condition of the material, he said, "It's worth the cost of cleaning solution to see you make something out of this."

The question of what the material would be used for was soon answered. It was to be made into a fur-trimmed, princess-style coat for me. I know that my mother had long wanted to make me a coat similar to the one in an ad for a Shirley Temple movie. When my mother first saw the ad, she carefully cut it out of the paper and placed it in her sewing basket. At last, she had most of the basic material she needed to make it. As she explained to my father, the problem was that there was just not enough of the good material to cut the pattern. At first, she appeared not to hear my father when he asked, "Why can't you make it two-tone?"

As his words sunk in, she stopped turning the pattern pieces and responded, "Why can't I make it two-tone?"

By the time I went to bed, the dining room floor was littered with wool garments of every color and description. My last view of my mother that evening was of her holding a ladies' black wool chinchilla jacket up to the light. As my father watched her over the rims of his reading glasses, she nodded her head and smiled.

The next morning there was no sign of the black jacket, but that afternoon the disassembled jacket was laid out on the dining room table with several pattern pieces firmly attached. All that evening my mother shifted material and pattern pieces in an effort to complete the layout. Finally, she was satisfied that she had made the optimum use of the available material. We all held our breath as she began to cut out the coat. We knew that one slip of the scissors and my vision of wearing a Shirley Temple style coat would fall to pieces. At last, we were able to exhale, as she finished cutting the last piece of the coat.

The incident of the red-and-black chinchilla coat taught me that miracles do not come easy. There were many long nights of labor as my mother began to assemble the coat. Once she had determined that it could be made, she set the deadline for completion at Christmas Eve. She was determined that I would wear the coat to the church program on Christmas Sunday.

It would be impossible to describe the various techniques and innovations my mother used in making that coat. In the end, she produced a gorgeous garment— a princess-style coat with front and back yokes of black wool chinchilla, trimmed with collar and cuffs of gray fox, and lined with black satin, which was recovered from a pair of my uncle's pajamas. It was a coat that would have done Shirley Temple proud. Uncle Smitty said, "Marvin glows when she wears that coat."

My uncle was right. That coat did something for me that no other garment had ever done. It made me feel beautiful. I wore it to the Christmas program and received the anticipated flood of compliments. While some of the ladies did not comment, they were unable to resist touching the soft fur collar and cuffs. My mother stood back, taking it all in. I had never seen her happier.

I wore the coat to church on Sundays and on rare special occasions. If my mother would let me, I would have worn it everyday. My father seemed concerned that I might be getting a big head. He pulled me aside and explained that I had the coat only because my mother was an artist with a needle. While he wanted me to enjoy wearing it, he also wanted me to realize that it didn't make me better than anyone else, that it was what was in my mind and heart that had value, not what I had on my back. I nodded my head yes, but at the age of twelve, I realized that he was a man and did not understand.

When the day came, and it had to come, that I asked permission to wear the coat to school, my mother was prepared. She explained that it was a dress coat to be worn only to church and on special occasions, never to school. I sulked for a few days but finally forgot about the coat. There were other exciting things to think about. Miss Barnett, our music teacher, had obtained a block of tickets for a performance of the Nutcracker Suite, to be performed at the Masonic Temple. In addition to teaching music at Sill School, Miss Barnett gave private piano lessons and had many friends in the entertainment world. The tickets were distributed based on scholastic accomplishment, and my name was near the top of the list.

You would have thought the school management would be delighted with the gift of tickets, but the opposite proved true. The head of the art department, Mrs. Grant, voiced the common sentiment when she said, "That Miss Barnett and her Bohemian friends are turning this school into a guinea pig for their own social experiments."

While we did not fully understand the meaning of this statement, we did sense the disapproval of Miss Barnett that it implied. Experiment or not, we were all excited about attending the performance. Even our parents were excited by the prospect.

Although happy about the outing, my mother was torn between the need to insure that I was properly dressed for the occasion and her desire to go to Canada with Aunt Bessie. Whenever Uncle Chuck was home for a few days from his shift on the railroad, he would take Aunt Bessie and my mother to Windsor to spend the day. They would leave early in the morning and return that night. Uncle Chuck would drop them off at a large market on the main street of Windsor and return to pick them up about six o'clock in the evening. Footloose and fancy-free, my aunt and mother would roam downtown Windsor like two children at play. Mrs. Eubanks had gone with them once but had declared them "too silly for me" and never went again.

These trips usually took place on a Saturday, but this time Friday was the only day Uncle Chuck had free. It happened to be the same Friday scheduled for the ballet. What a dilemma! Mrs. Eubanks was the only person, other than Aunt Bessie, who my mother felt comfortable asking favors of, and she was visiting her daughter down south. My father, knowing how much these trips meant to my mother, volunteered to take a half-day off from work to see that I was properly dressed for the occasion. My mother laid out my clothes the night before, including my gray school jacket. My father's job was to make sure that I washed up and brushed my hair before leaving.

When I arrived home at noon that Friday, my father had the washbasin, soap, and towels laid out. After I finished the wash-up, he decided to brush my hair to make sure it was done right. I almost laughed out loud at the awkward way he raked the brush across my hair. When he had finished, I went into my mother's bedroom and corrected the damage he had done.

After dressing, I picked up my gray jacket and headed out of the bedroom for a final inspection by my father. Suddenly, I hesitated—genius had struck again! My mother had said that the red-and-black chinchilla coat was to be worn only to church and on special occasions. Surely, a trip to a matinee at the Masonic Temple qualified as a truly special occasion. Filled with a sense of righteous virtue, I threw the gray jacket back on the bed, reached into the closet, and pulled out that gorgeous red-and-black chinchilla coat. It was only fair to my mother that I wear it.

When Uncle Chuck dropped my mother off at about eight o'clock that evening, I was still regaling my father with the details of the day: the beautiful costumes, the dancing, the music, even the ice cream sodas Miss Barnett had treated the group to after the performance. It was not until years later that my father described how Miss Barnett had prevailed upon her uncle, the owner of an ice cream parlor on Linwood Avenue, to close up for an hour so that she could safely treat her racially mixed group to sodas. He learned about it through the ever-efficient grapevine, as one of the Bower boys worked as a janitor at Snyder's Ice Cream Parlor.

With my mother's arrival, I gained my second wind and repeated the whole description, omitting not even the smallest detail. After being constantly assured that I had looked my finest that afternoon, my mother went into her bedroom to hang up her coat and hat. There, lying on the bed, in full view, was the red-and-black chinchilla coat. I knew, immediately, that I was in deep trouble. Why, oh, why hadn't I hung that coat back up in the closet? I watched as the color drained from my mother's face. In a voice just above a whisper, she asked, "William, will you please come here?"

It must have been the tone, not the volume of her voice, that propelled him from his chair. As I stood trembling in fear, he asked, "What's wrong, Gracie?" When she did not immediately reply, he asked again, "Is something wrong?"

Looking at my guilty face, she responded, "Only if Marvin wore this coat to the matinee."

My father looked at her in bewilderment and asked, "Isn't that the coat you laid out? I told Marvin to wash up and get dressed, and I thought she put on the clothes you laid out for her. It is her best coat, and I thought you would want her to wear it."

Something shriveled inside me as I watched my mother's face crumple like a dishrag and tears spring to her eyes. In a sad voice, she looked at both of us and said, "You don't understand what you've done. I'll never get another used garment from Marvin's teachers. They don't mind giving you things to be made into plain, everyday clothes, but they don't want to see something they gave you made into a coat fit for one of Rockefeller's children. Why do you think I take the crochet collar and cuffs off the dresses I let Marvin wear to school? I can kiss her teachers goodbye as a source of material."

My father scoffed at my mother's statement, but her words proved true. The supply of used garments dried up much like water dries up when the sun hits it. For awhile, the teachers even stopped bringing garments to my mother for repair and alteration. This did not last long, though, because their salaries did not allow them to indulge their prejudices in that way. The flow of used clothing, however, did not resume.

What followed confirmed the truth of that old saying, "When one door closes, another door opens."

One day, Miss Barnett gave me a bag to take home to my mother. The bag was filled with used garments. Some were obviously Miss Barnett's, but there were even men's shirts and pants. Mother said, "Maybe the other teachers have done us a favor. Everything in the bag is made of fine quality material and carries name brand labels."

As far as I was concern, Miss Barnett's contribution to our wardrobes was not the only good thing to come out of a bad situation. My mother told me I could wear that red-and-black chinchilla coat with the fur collar and cuffs to school any day I wanted to. And I did.

WHEN YOUR GODS
HAVE FEET OF CLAY

Miss Marjorie Reynolds came to teach at Sill School in the fall of 1939. It was rumored that she was a distant cousin of the Reynolds tobacco family. The rumor, whether true or not, did add a certain glamour to her arrival. It was not that Miss Reynolds needed additional glamour. With her long blonde hair, crepe chiffon outfits, and dainty three-inch heels, she appeared more like a movie star than a novice grade school teacher in a racially mixed neighborhood.

From the beginning, it was obvious that Miss Reynolds was altogether different from the other teachers at Sill School. For starters, she insisted on addressing each student as miss or mister and requested that we do the same with each other. We felt very grown-up and sophisticated and began to use *please* and *thank you* more often than normal. In a few short weeks, our homeroom became the model for the school. Whenever board of education dignitaries visited the school, our homeroom was pointed out for special recognition. This turn of events instantly endeared Miss Reynolds to the front office but quickly alienated her from most of the female teachers at Sill School. As much as the teachers disliked her, the students of her fifth grade homeroom loved her.

When my father asked about my new teacher, I responded with lavish praise and descriptions of our classroom format. He nodded his head in agreement until I mentioned the requirement that the students use the titles miss and mister, then a small frown creased his forehead.

He stared off into the distance for a few seconds and then said, "Maybe I had better have a little talk with this Miss Reynolds."

Mother sighed and cautioned my father that "it might be best to leave well enough alone."

A month passed before Father had an opportunity to have that "little talk" with Miss Reynolds.

He set up an appointment to see her after school on a Friday. In an obvious attempt to heed my mother's warnings, he first congratulated her on her teaching methods, then asked if she was aware of his mandate that his children not be forced to use the titles sir or ma'am. Before Miss Reynolds could respond, he suggested that perhaps our current use of the titles miss or mister came dangerously close to crossing that line.

During the long pause that followed, I sat with my head down and eyes tightly closed. I knew all too well how easily Father could reduce a teacher to a state of tongue-tied nervousness. In a way, it was this ability that most endeared him to me, but this time it was different. Miss Reynolds was special, and I was torn between loyalty to my father and affection for her. Then, she began to speak in the same soft, calm voice she used with her students.

Only the rhythmic tapping of one foot betrayed her tension as she said, "Mr. Sprague, I agree with your dislike for the automatic usage of titles such as sir and ma'am by our Negro students. At best it smacks of a plantation mentality, and at worst it's downright patronizing. However, that is a far cry from having the students use the titles miss or mister. First of all, they like it. It also serves as a great equalizer. Many of my students do not have a father and mother living at home; in fact, many of them do not have any parents and are living with relatives. The use of the titles puts everyone on an equal footing."

That afternoon, I was witness to something I had never seen before and would never see again—my father at a loss for words. Finally, he collected his thoughts and said, "When you present it like that, it makes a good deal of sense. It's just that I have to be very careful when it comes to my children."

Miss Reynolds nodded her agreement, and the meeting ended.

On the walk home, I hummed quietly to myself as I double-skipped in an effort to keep up with my father. He was curiously silent and seemed engrossed in deep thought. When Mother saw the smiles on our faces, she breathed a sigh of relief. When she asked my father what he thought of my teacher, he answered, "Well, she may be one of those bleeding heart liberals, but she's certainly a sincere one. I think she'll be good for the children."

For the next year and a half, peace and quiet reigned between my father and the school. I was in seventh heaven. Two of my most favorite people in the world, my father and Miss Reynolds, liked and respected each other. How could anything go wrong? Unfortunately, I had forgotten the favorite saying of our resident busybody, Mrs. Hodges. "Bad luck follows good luck, like night follows day. Why, it's the law of nature," she would say.

I didn't know much about the laws of nature, but disaster did strike during the first week of the new school term.

It's ironic how trouble often rides in on the back of good intentions. So it was with the events that led to the demise of my relationship with Miss Reynolds. The term began on a high note, as Miss Reynolds was to serve not only as our home-room teacher but our social studies teacher as well. The structure of each social studies class was left to the individual teacher. Our course was a hodgepodge of history and literature.

It was the history portion of the class that most intrigued me. The scandals of the European courts seemed not unlike the scandals that so often consumed our neighborhood. It was my love of history that was to serve as the gateway to the most traumatic experience of my young life.

I do not recall the exact content of the history lesson that fateful Monday morning. I do remember that it had something to do with an argument between the King of Sweden and his court officials. During the lesson, Miss Reynolds used the expression "something is rotten in the state of Denmark."

When she realized we did not understand the expression, she attempted to explain its meaning.

She began her explanation by saying, "I'm sure everyone in this room has had the experience of feeling that something was just not right, although you didn't know exactly what was wrong. That is what the expression means."

When we still appeared puzzled, Miss Reynolds undertook to further explain the meaning of the expression. To this day, I wish that she had left us in complete ignorance, but fate had other plans. She hesitated for a moment, then said, "Perhaps you will understand if I use the American expression that means the same thing." Then, with a face illuminated only by a sincere desire to impart knowledge, she uttered those fateful words, "You'll always find a nigger in the woodpile."

In the silence that followed, that WORD echoed and re-echoed around the room. As Miss Reynolds realized the impact of her words on the class, she half rose from her chair and gestured wildly with her hands in what appeared a vain attempt to recapture the words from the empty air. I looked on in disbelief as she turned on her heels and fled the room.

The class sat in stunned silence. Looking around the room, I could feel the unspoken question directed at me, "What should we do?"

For once, I didn't have the answer but could only follow Miss Reynolds's example and flee the room.

I don't know how I reached home. I know that I must have run down Herbert Street, crossed Thirtieth Street, Twenty-eighth Street, and Lovett Avenue, but I have no memory of doing so. I remember crossing Scotten Avenue only because of the horns that blared as several cars narrowly avoided hitting me. Finally, I arrived home, ran up the back steps, and threw myself into my mother's arms.

After all attempts to calm me failed, Mother became very alarmed. She hurried next door to ask Mrs. Eubanks to come and stay with me while she went to the school to find out what in the world had happened. On the corner of Herbert and Lovett, she met Mrs. Pringle, the vice principal, hurrying toward our house.

Upon returning home, my mother bundled me into her large four-poster bed. Its two mattresses leveled the bed with the window overlooking Herbert Street. As dusk fell and the streetlights came on, a calm settled over me, and I drifted into a deep sleep.

I don't know where my parents slept that night, or if they slept at all. I only know that when I awoke in the morning, Father had already left for work, and Mother was in the kitchen fixing my breakfast. The only other time I had been served breakfast in bed was the day I returned from the hospital after having my tonsils removed. Lying in my parent's bed, I felt safe and secure from the outside world that could so easily betray me. All that day I drifted in and out of sleep, finally waking to the sound of my father's voice and the fevered gold of an evening sunset.

The next morning, when my father asked, "Wouldn't you like to talk with Miss Reynolds so the two of you can iron out the situation," I was surprised.

How could my father ask such a question? How could a "race man" like my father, a man as loyal to his race as to his God, believe that I would ever want to see that woman again? She had betrayed me! Made me the laughing stock of my class! I would never forgive her!

After several moments of silence, my father said, "Marvin, I'm afraid I've failed you. I only wanted to teach you how to tell good from evil. It seems that I've actually succeeded in teaching you the same intolerance I've fought against all of my life!"

Then he sighed and left the room, closing the door behind him.

For the next two days, I remained secluded in my parents' bedroom while turning a deaf ear to my father's entreaties to forgive and forget. When Miss Reynolds came and tapped on the bedroom door, begging me to open up and at least listen to what she had to say, I did not respond. Even when I heard her ask Father to speak for her, I turned my face to the wall, stuck a finger in each ear, and hummed, loudly, to drown out the sound of his voice. Despite my best efforts, I did hear her footsteps moving through the kitchen and out the back door.

After she left, my father entered the bedroom and said what proved to be his final words on the matter. He said, "Marvin, you will live to regret this day."

When I returned to school the next Monday, I had been moved to another homeroom and dropped from Miss Reynolds's social studies class. No one mentioned the incident, and everything appeared to return to normal. At home, we resumed the normal rhythm of our lives. I saw very little of Miss Reynolds the balance of the term, because I began to use the side door to enter and leave school.

On Sunday morning, December 7, 1941, an event occurred that drove all thoughts of Miss Reynolds from my mind. The attack on Pearl Harbor was not only exciting but also awoke in me a sense of patriotism I did not know I had. In the midst of all the confusion, it was announced that Miss Reynolds would not return to Sill School after the Christmas holidays. The words went in one ear and out the other.

THE GREAT FEET WASHINGS

uring the week before Easter, activity in our neighborhood reached fever pitch. Preparations for the Easter parade were in full flow. Next to Christmas, Easter was the holiday that best defined a family's level of prosperity. Easter outfits were often put in layaway as early as January to ensure that the entire family was appropriately dressed on Easter morning. A fortunate few, with prosperous relatives in other cities, received gifts of money to assist in the gala preparations. Nothing was wasted. Outgrown Easter outfits were passed down in families or given to close friends. Each year there was a frenzied rush to be the first to lay claim to any current Easter outfits that might be outgrown by the next year. In addition, preparations for another Easter ceremony was on-going, a ceremony that my father referred to as the Great Feet Washings.

The feet washing ceremony took place on Good Friday evening. Members of the Church of the True Believers would gather to physically wash one another's feet just as Jesus Christ washed the feet of his disciples. The choice of date and time was not accidental. The congregation believed that this most humble of acts was a fitting end to a day that symbolically celebrated the crucifixion of our Lord and Savior, Jesus Christ, who died on the Cross to save the sinner from his sins. What the Easter parade was to the children, the feet washing ceremony was to the adults.

In many ways, the ceremony was as much a theatrical event as a religious rit-ual. The participants would arrive at the church in street clothes, enter the robing room, and emerge draped in white sheets. They covered their heads with white scarves of every imaginable design. There were crocheted scarves, embroidered scarves, ribbon-edged scarves, silk scarves, and just plain white cotton scarves. A large white towel was draped over each shoulder. Every article had to be whiter than white. No matter how white the items were, they were never considered white enough. There was an unspoken contest among the ladies as to who would wear the whitest garments. It was as if the whiter the garment, the purer the act.

As Good Friday approached, a dramatic change came over the neighborhood. Washtubs were dragged out and set on bricks in backyards. Fires were lit under them, and the tubs were filled with water, carbolic soap, and heavy doses of Roman Cleanser Bleach. After washing, the sheets and towels that would be worn to the ceremony were dumped into this mixture. Usually, they would soak all day and all night. The next morning they would be thoroughly rinsed and hung on the clothesline to dry. Once, Sister English soaked her sheets and towels so long in the bleach mixture that when she finally rinsed them, they came apart in her hands.

Although Mother scrubbed her sheets and towels with Fels Naphtha Soap, she never made an all out effort to whiten her garments. It wasn't because she didn't want to. It was because she knew Father would tease her, unmercifully, if he found her competing in the unofficial contest. On the one day that she ventured to boil the articles in bleach, my father came home early. "Well, Gracie," he said, "I see you're getting ready for your annual act of humility. You ladies are really storing up treasures in heaven. There'll be plenty of stars in your heavenly crowns. You would think that getting into heaven depended on how white the garments are that you'll wear at the ceremony. Wonder if the gentlemen are somewhere bleaching their clothes?"

Although the few male members of the congregation held a separate feet washing ceremony in the cloakroom of the church, it was common knowledge that they substituted a Bible class for the ceremony and no feet were washed.

When I was twelve years old, Mother decided I was old enough to attend the ceremony. When I asked, "Mama, can Beatrice come with us," my mother said, "I'm sorry, Marvin, only the daughters of members taking part in the ceremony may attend."

From across the room, my father let out a snort and asked, "Who made that rule? Is that another act of humility?"

My mother didn't respond, but later that evening I heard her tell Aunt Bessie that she thought my father was right. "What difference does it make if Beatrice comes along," she said. "It's not her fault that her mother drinks and her father abuses the family. Reverend Elder should stand up to the hypocrites in the congregation!"

Aunt Bessie laughed and said, "You'd better not let Bill hear you say that. You'll never live it down."

About seven o'clock on Good Friday evening, my mother and I started out for church. Swinging out the front gate, we joined a steady stream of women and girls headed for the Church of the True Believers. Everyone was in a festive mood and dressed in her best bib and tucker. I had on my Easter dress from the previous year, and my hair was braided so tightly that my forehead was rimmed with pressure bumps. Each braid wore its own ribbon. All in all, I was quite pleased with the way I looked. The ladies carried their freshly washed and pressed garments carefully over their forearms. Some garments were starched so heavily that they were difficult to carry and gave off a rustling sound as they rubbed against each other.

When we reached the steps of the church, a deadly silence fell over the crowd. Reverend Elder stood in the doorway dressed in a long white robe, her hair covered by a white lace kerchief drawn low over her forehead and tied in a knot at the nape of her neck. As we entered the church, the pianist softly played the hymn "And He Never Said A Mumbling Word."

We marched down the center aisle to the front of the church, separating as we came to the front row of pews. The women filed into the robing room, and we girls took seats in the front pews. How proud we were to be taking part in the ceremony. Attendance at this ceremony was considered a major step on the road to womanhood.

The ladies returned decked out in their whiter-than-snow garments and took up their positions in the row of chairs that had been placed in front of the altar facing the congregation. The first lady to the far left of the altar held a small foot basin in her lap and wore a large white towel draped across her shoulder. Reverend Elder stood at the pulpit with her Bible opened to the book of St. John. In a solemn voice, she called out, "John 13:5. May the Lord add a blessing to the reading of his word."

In ringing tones, she read the verses that described Jesus washing his disciples' feet. Looking out over the audience, she said, "With this humble action, Jesus demonstrated that we are all God's children. With this ceremony, we recommit ourselves to our Lord and Savior, Jesus Christ."

Then the ceremony began. The woman to the far left of the altar knelt down in front of the woman to her right and placed the small basin, filled halfway with water, on the floor before her. Lifting first one and then the other foot, she immersed them in the water. A quick swish of the water, then each foot was lifted and dried with the towel she pulled from her shoulder. When she had finished, she retook her seat, while the second woman washed the feet of the woman to her right. Slowly, one by one, this act of humility was repeated over and over again. The last woman in the row washed Reverend Elder's feet, and the Reverend, in turn, washed the feet of the woman who started the cycle.

The completion of the circle ended the ceremony. Reverend Elder gave a short benediction, and we filed quietly out of the church and went our separate ways.

For the next three years, I faithfully attended the feet washing ceremonies. With each ceremony, I gained a better understanding of the true meaning of the act. I realized that the ability to perform this humble, and in some ways demeaning, act demonstrated true strength of character. I looked forward to the day when I would become an active participant in the ceremony. That day, however, never came.

Over the years, Mother frequently commented on the decline in the number of women who participated in the ceremony, but I never noticed. She blamed it on the war and continual prosperity. Like Aunt Bessie said, "It's hard to be humble when you have paychecks laying on the dresser that you don't have time to cash."

On Good Friday, 1943, only three members showed up for the ceremony, my mother, my aunt, and Reverend Elder. That day marked not only the end of the feet washing ceremonies but also the end of much that was good and true at the Church of the True Believers.

THE VOTE

I never knew Mr. Eubanks. He passed away before I was born. He had worked for the railroad, and it was rumored that Mrs. Eubanks received a substantial pension check every month. I did meet the Eubanks girls, Nettie and Gladys, on one of their infrequent visits to their mother, who, next to my family and Aunt Bessie, held the strongest grip on my heart. Children know when they are loved, and Mrs. Eubanks loved me.

Oddly enough, competition for her affection came not from her children but from the most unlikely source, the president of the United States, Franklin Delano Roosevelt. My father once said, "Mr. Eubanks was a lucky man. He had the good fortune to die before his wife fell in love with President Roosevelt."

Exactly when Mrs. Eubanks developed this affection, which bordered on obsession, was never determined. My father first noticed it midway through President Roosevelt's second term. She would come by daily, after supper, to ask my father if there were any news of Mr. Roosevelt in the paper that day. When he would reply no, a look of disappointment would cross her face. If he responded yes, she would plop down beside him and patiently wait for him to find the paper and read the article to her. She would savor every word, often asking him to reread those passages that were most flattering to the president.

At first, people in the neighborhood teased Mrs. Eubanks about the president. Some even took to referring to President Roosevelt as her boyfriend. The quiet but dignified way she responded left no doubt in anyone's mind what she thought of such antics. All such references soon subsided.

As the 1940 presidential election drew near, the flow of newspaper articles referencing the president increased. When it was reported that President Roosevelt would run for an unprecedented third term, the media exploded. Debates were held on radio. Editorials took over a larger portion of the newsprint. The pros

and cons raged back and forth. On the evening the *Detroit News* reported that running for a third presidential term, although it had never been done before, was neither illegal nor fattening, Mrs. Eubanks laughed outright with glee. Father always said that was the night that the germ of an idea formed in her mind.

The jury was still out on the question of whether Mrs. Eubanks could read or write. The manager of Weinstein's Grocery and Vegetable Market, where she cashed her widow's pension check, said he had seen her sign her name as clear as day. Other tradespeople on Warren Avenue swore that she could neither read nor write but used an X to signify signature. It was my father who finally put the issue to rest by saying, "Mrs. Eubanks has a limited ability to read and write."

The next Sunday, Mrs. Eubanks stopped by after church. It was the conversation she held with my father that proved most unusual. At first speaking in a whisper, but gaining volume as her courage increased, she said, "Mr. Sprague, you know I usually don't ask favors, but I need a favor now."

Later, Father would say that it was the sincerity in her voice that stayed the flippant response he was about to make. Instead, he leaned forward and said, "Mrs. Eubanks, you know if there's anything I can do for you, you have only to ask. Why, you're like family!"

Mrs. Eubanks stared long and hard into my father's eyes. Then, as if reassured by what she saw there, she broached the subject that was the real reason for her visit. "Mr. Sprague, you know I can read and write some. I do pretty well if I take my time, but for what I want to do, that's not good enough. I want to register and vote for President Roosevelt in the next election."

Father leaned back in his chair and took a deep breath before he responded, "Mrs. Eubanks, I'll be proud to help you qualify to vote in the next election."

My father approached preparing Mrs. Eubanks to qualify to vote the same way an army general prepares for an impending battle. He appointed my brother as her reading coach. He put out feelers all over the neighborhood for anyone who might have written information about the registration process. Nothing happened. In desperation, he finally asked a local alderman for help. The next day, the alderman dropped off a sealed envelope for my father. Inside were copies of the ballot and registration forms used in the 1936 general election.

Armed with this material, school began in earnest. Over the next three weeks, Mrs. Eubanks spent evening hours at our house being tutored by my father and brother. The going was tough. My mother and I would sit in the living room beaming positive thoughts at the figures hunched over the dining room table. Night after night, Father mumbled in frustration as Mrs. Eubanks moved three steps forward and four steps back in the learning process. Only my mother appeared confident that she would vote in the general election.

The solution to the problem proved to be very simple and came about by accident. One evening, Mother and Aunt Bessie sat at the kitchen table discussing what, if anything, they could do to help Mrs. Eubanks reach her goal. My father's frustration had reached the point where he was considering telling her he couldn't help her after all. It was barely two weeks to the election, and her reading and comprehension skills had increased only slightly. After a prolonged silence, Aunt Bessie said, "If we could just get her to see it. Maybe if she could picture the words in her mind, she would understand them."

"That's it!" my mother exclaimed. "They say a picture is worth a thousand words. We need to draw her a picture."

When Mother described what she had in mind to Father, he was as excited as she was. That evening, instead of giving Mrs. Eubanks a reading lesson, he took a sheet of paper and began to draw. On one side he drew a picture of a donkey, and on the reverse a picture of an elephant. Then he circled the picture of the donkey that appeared to the left of the Democratic Party listing on the sample ballot. "Mrs. Eubanks," he said, "I promised you would vote, and vote you will. You already know how to fill out the registration forms. All you have to know to vote the straight Democratic ticket is where to place your X on the ballot. Just place it opposite the picture of the donkey, and you'll have cast a vote for President Roosevelt and all the other Democratic nominees!"

Election day dawned cold and clear. Long before the polls opened, Mrs. Eubanks sat at our kitchen table drinking a cup of my father's strong black coffee. I awoke to the sound of her voice saying, "Mr. Sprague, I don't know whether I can go through with it. I haven't been this nervous since Mr. Eubanks died!"

My father made the clucking sounds that people often make to calm a baby and said, "Don't worry, you'll do just fine. After all, I'll be there."

My mother took up her vigil. As she prepared breakfast for my brother and me, she stopped often to look at the wall clock and wonder aloud, "Where could she be? What's taking so long?"

It was not until my father returned from work that evening that we learned the true story of the great vote. The voting precinct was housed in Lothrop Library. As my father and Mrs. Eubanks climbed the steps, he could feel her begin to shake violently. He almost carried her to the registration desk, where the clerk checked to see if her name was on the voting rolls. So far, so good. The clerk handed Mrs.

Eubanks a ballot and pointed her toward an empty booth. As Mrs. Eubanks raised the curtain to the booth, she suddenly stopped, turned to my father, and said, "I'm sorry, Mr. Sprague, I just can't do it."

Even as he described the scene, a look came over Father's face that must have mimicked the look he wore at that moment. When Mother asked him what he did, he answered, "What did I do? I didn't know what to do. I just stood there in shock."

Suddenly, he sensed motion behind him and turned to look directly into the face of Mrs. Blanchard, head librarian at Lothrop Library. Giving him the slightest of winks, she said, "Mr. Sprague, of course you know since Mrs. Eubanks is handicapped, you can accompany her into the booth to assist her in voting. Isn't that true, Mrs. David?"

The registration clerk, Mrs. David, looked from Mrs. Blanchard to Mrs. Eubanks to my father in confusion. "Why, yes, if she's handicapped, someone may assist her to vote."

Breathing a sigh of relief, Father took Mrs. Eubanks by the arm, and they entered the voting booth and drew the curtain behind them.

That is how Annie Louise Eubanks came to vote for President Roosevelt in his bid for an unprecedented third term. Little did she know that four years later, she would storm the polls to vote for him in his equally successful bid for a fourth.

SOPHISTICATED LADY

Whenever anyone mentioned Uncle Smitty and Aunt Freddie, my mother would laugh and say, "Your aunt should change her name to Frankie and your uncle should change his name to Johnnie. They act more like the man and woman in that old blues song than husband and wife."

I had no idea who Frankie and Johnnie were, but I did know that meeting and marrying my aunt was the best thing to happen to my uncle in a long, long time. I could tell Father agreed because of the way he spoke about Aunt Freddie. Whenever he referred to her, he always added, "At least she's intelligent enough to think for herself, which is more than I can say for the other women he's married."

Aunt Freddie was my uncle's fourth, or was it fifth, wife. It was hard to keep track. I had met the last two but could not really say that I knew them. My uncle had never remained married to any of them long enough for us to know them well.

I met Aunt Freddie for the first time on the day after Labor Day in 1940. School had started that day, and I was at Lothrop Library getting a head start on a history reading assignment. Miss Reynolds was our social studies teacher for the term, and I was anxious to get a good grade in her class. Once I met my new aunt, all thoughts of school and books disappeared from my mind.

As my brother later told me, "Your mouth was literally hanging open."

I had never before seen a woman who looked like Aunt Freddie. I had seen women who were prettier, slimmer, and younger but none as attractive as Aunt Freddie. It wasn't something that I could single out but a combination of all her qualities that made her a most sophisticated lady.

Dressed in a riding outfit, consisting of dark brown jodhpurs, a beige-and-white tweed jacket, a white silk shirt, and brown leather riding boots, she looked like a creature from another world. With a brown felt bowler hat atop her head and a short riding crop hanging from her waistband, she looked as if she had just stepped from the pages of *Vogue*.

I was her willing slave from the moment I saw her.

When my father discovered that she had traveled extensively in Europe, an instant rapport was established. My father seemed almost boyish as he and Aunt Freddie compared notes on similar dilemmas they had experienced while traveling abroad.

My mother was temporarily won over when Aunt Freddie praised the beauty and workmanship of her handmade quilts. Her ardor cooled, however, when my aunt mentioned that she had recently worked as a supervising seamstress for a prominent American dress designer.

In the fall of 1940, my world was in good order. I had Miss Reynolds, my favorite teacher at school, and Aunt Freddie, my favorite aunt at home. The fact that jobs at the downtown luxury hotels had dried up mattered little to me. It did, however, mean a great deal to my parents. The Depression was nearing its end, and like most contagious diseases, its effects became more evident as it gasped its last breath.

When chefs at several prominent downtown hotels learned of my father's plight, they banded together to give him rotational kitchen assignments to help him stay afloat. While these part-time jobs were helpful, the day came when our family had to bow to the inevitable and go on welfare. My father descended into the depths of despair. When he was assigned to manage a welfare storage facility, he cheered up. Our neighborhood was soon drowning in a sea of welfare commodities.

If these were dark days for my parents, they were bright days for their children. William was enrolled in an advance math class at Northwestern High School, and I was a member of the Sill School Verse Speaking Choir, formed by Miss Reynolds in conjunction with the school's art department. Math was my brother's love; anything involving Miss Reynolds was my joy. Together, my brother and I continued to attend Saturday afternoon matinees at the Rogers Theater and enjoy Sunday afternoon drives around Belle Isle with my aunt and uncle.

One hot, sticky evening, Aunt Freddie came by to take us for a drive. Uncle Smitty was in Chicago at a meeting of the Brotherhood of Sleeping Car Porters and Maids. My uncle was neither a porter nor a maid, but he believed that, if the brotherhood gained better working conditions and higher wages for its members, the effects would trickle down to improve the lot of the railway maintenance crews.

When my aunt came in, Mother gave Father an odd look. Aunt Freddie looked very strange. Her hair was uncombed, and her clothes were rumpled. When she bent to hug me, I smelled a sour, fishy odor. I drew back in surprise because I had always enjoyed her hugs, in part, because of the freshness of her breath and the sweet scent of the perfume she wore.

My aunt told us to hurry up and get ready to go, but Father interrupted her, saying, "Freddie, I don't think they can go with you this evening. They haven't finished their homework yet."

When she attempted to persuade him to let us go anyway, my father took her by the arm and almost dragged her out to her car. He put her into the passenger seat, then went around to the driver's side, got in, and drove off. As Mother watched from the living room window, she mumbled to herself, "How dare she come here in that condition! I don't care what your father says, I don't want her to come here again!"

My brother and I went outside and sat on the front steps. Something was very wrong with Aunt Freddie, and my mother and father were upset with her. We didn't know what she had done to anger them. We only knew that she was our Aunt Freddie, and right or wrong, we loved her just the same.

When Father returned, he and Mother went into the house and closed the door. As Mother paced back and forth in the living room, we listened at the open window.

"William, you will have to talk to her," she said. "We have never exposed the children to anything like that, and we're certainly not going to start now."

The only words we heard from Father were, "Yes, Gracie, I know."

The next Sunday afternoon, my aunt and uncle visited as usual. Aunt Freddie was her usual stylish self, and when she bent to hug me, I was again enveloped in clouds of Chanel N° 5. Oh, happy day! Everything appeared back to normal.

My uncle continued to come faithfully every Sunday afternoon to take us for a ride, but now my aunt was often among the missing. When Mother asked about her, my uncle would say things like, "Oh, she went to Chicago to visit a girl-friend," or, "She's helping out in the preparations for a fashion show."

Mother would usually respond with a "how nice" and promptly drop the subject.

Finally, after a prolonged absence by Aunt Freddie, my uncle admitted to Father that he and Freddie had separated. Not long after this announcement, Father told us that Uncle Smitty had filed for divorce.

Our family had helped my uncle through several divorces, but this time was different. Father said, "Gracie, I feel like I'm losing a good friend. You can say what you want to about Freddie, but she's different from the rest. She's had a hard life. Deep down she's a decent person. It's too bad that she had to get mixed up with a drinking crowd. Take it from me, liquor and Indian blood just don't mix."

My mother responded, "I know William. Freddie can make me angry enough to slap her face, but I love her just the same."

As for my brother, all was gloom. He was a very quiet person who held his feelings inside. When he heard that my aunt and uncle were divorcing, he momentarily dropped his guard and actually shed a few tears. As for me, I was openly inconsolable.

When Uncle Smitty showed up on the Monday before his court date, we did our best to be upbeat. He had come, he said, to make sure Bill would be able to appear in court the next day.

Father seemed surprised by the request but responded, "I'd rather not take a day off from work, but if you feel you need moral support, I will."

"Moral support," my uncle responded, "you are going to testify for me, aren't you?"

"Testify to what?" Father asked.

"Testify that you have personal knowledge that Freddie was a poor wife, that she is a drunk who cannot be trusted. Verify that I spent time and money in a desperate attempt to get her to kick the habit. Testify about how good I was to her and how she repaid my goodness with lies and deceit."

It was then that Father lost his temper. "Testify that she's an alcoholic," he erupted. "Yes, she's an alcoholic, but you knew that from the beginning! You courted her with Johnny Walker Red Label! You've never taken her anywhere but bars and nightclubs! What did you expect? You knew what she was when you married her! She never lied to you! And now that you've given up on her, you want me to turn on her so that you can gain your freedom! No, Smitty! I don't think I can do that. Not even for you!"

A deadly silence followed this outburst. It was broken when my mother said, "You've both said things you don't really mean. Let's sleep on the matter and discuss it again tomorrow."

In a steely voice, my uncle said, "We don't have to sleep on it. Just answer me one question, Bill. Are you going to testify on my behalf or not?"

In a voice laced with sadness, my father said, "No."

After my uncle left, Mother attempted to reason with Father. She reminded him that Smitty was blood, and his request deserved special consideration. Father listened, patiently, to every word she said and then attempted to explain how he felt about the situation.

"Gracie, I wish I could, but I can't," he said. "It would be the same as lying. I can't preach the value of honesty to my children and not practice it myself."

Mother saw that she was fighting a losing battle, so she gave up the fight and returned to her mending. I believe that in her heart, she agreed with my father.

While my parents wrestled with the Freddie problem, I found myself on the horns of a different dilemma. I agreed with my father's stand but for an entirely different reason. My uncle was asking Father to testify against Aunt Freddie—Aunt Freddie, who gave me perfumed sachets for my dresser drawers; Aunt Freddie, who bought me satin ribbons for my hair and angora socks for my feet; Aunt Freddie, who never failed to greet me with a "Hi, Miss Pretty!"

The months went by with no word from my uncle. We did hear that the divorce was granted and that Aunt Freddie had moved back to Chicago without even a word of farewell. When Mother expressed surprise that she had not stopped by to say goodbye before leaving, Father answered, "Gracie, don't you understand? She didn't want to take the chance of breaking down before the children."

Some months later, a letter arrived for my father postmarked Chicago, Illinois. My mother said it was from Aunt Freddie. When Father got home from work, he read the letter. He did not read it aloud but folded it and put it in his wallet. The letter was never mentioned again.

Summer ended, and fall's brilliant colors covered the landscape. As hunting season approached, Father's spirits seemed to sink. One Friday evening, Uncle Smitty suddenly appeared at our backdoor. As if he and Father had parted only hours before, he said, "Bill, Old Man Pritchard said we can hunt his underbrush this year. We'd better get an early start. Say about five o'clock in the morning?"

Without missing a beat, Father replied, "Okay, but maybe 4:30 would be better."

GREATER LOVE HAS NO MAN

One day I arrived home from school to find Mr. Dickinson sitting in our living room surrounded by several pieces of luggage. He and my mother were talking in hushed tones, although they were the only ones in the house. As I entered through the back door, I heard my mother say, "William will be home in a little while, and he'll know what to do."

Mr. Dickinson did not speak but moaned, softly, and dropped his head into his hands.

When Mother noticed me standing in the doorway, she got up and pulled me into the kitchen, closing the door behind her. In a low voice she said, "Marvin, I want you to do exactly as I say. You are to spend the night with Mrs. Eubanks. Now don't ask any questions, just do as I say. I'll explain later."

With a final pat on the shoulder, she steered me down the back steps and toward Mrs. Eubanks's house.

Mrs. Eubanks seemed to sense my anxiety. She let me stay up as late as I pleased. She did not comment when I kept repeatedly going to her back door to peer across at my house. The light in our kitchen did not go out. It was still on when I finally fell asleep on Mrs. Eubanks's sofa.

Bright and early the next morning, Mother came to get me. Mrs. Eubanks had given me breakfast, braided my hair, and freshened the dress I had worn by ironing it lightly. When I went to get my schoolbooks, my mother steered me to my bedroom through the back hall as she said, "Let's be quiet, Mr. Dickinson is asleep on the day bed in the living room. He's been up nearly all night and needs some rest."

I rescued my books and went to the front porch to wait for Beatrice. What was taking Beatrice so long? If anyone could figure out what was going on, it would be Beatrice.

Beatrice did not fail me. Without missing a beat, she said, "Head in hands, pieces of luggage, it's obvious he's left home. He probably had a fight with his wife, and she threw him out. He won't be around long. They'll soon make up. I wouldn't be surprise to see a new baby by next year."

A sense of relief washed over me. If that was all it was, there was nothing to worry about. I thought someone had died.

My brother and I knew a great deal about Mr. Dickinson, and yet we knew nothing. My father had met him long before he met my mother, although the circumstances of that meeting were left unclear. We knew that he was a vice president at the U.S. Rubber Company, with offices in downtown Detroit. Occasionally, very occasionally, he would pull up outside in his long, black Chrysler, get out, and come in and talk to my father briefly. We also knew that my father had worked for him as a chauffeur a long time ago. We knew they were friends because Mr. Dickinson said they were friends. This statement really confused us, as we did not know of any other Negro who had a white person as a close friend. Since my father did not deny the statement, although he did look a little uncomfortable every time it was made, we accepted it as true. Our curiosity was really aroused when Mr. Dickinson asked, "Did your father ever tell you how he saved my life?"

It was at this point that my father balked. He looked at Mr. Dickinson and said, "Bob, I told you we would never speak of that again, especially before my children."

Mr. Dickinson blushed and said, "Sorry, Bill, it won't happen again. It's just that I can't forget that I wouldn't be here today if it weren't for you."

We tried to pry the story out of my mother, but she denied having any knowledge of the subject. When we persisted, she said, "I would tell you if I knew. That is the one thing your father will not discuss. If he won't tell me, he certainly isn't going to tell anyone else."

I think we accepted the truth of her statement, but time would prove us wrong. There was one other person who knew the story, Uncle Smitty. A time was fast approaching when he would feel compelled to use that knowledge to do what my father could not, or would not, do.

Several weeks went by and Mr. Dickinson remained secreted in the living room. Gradually, his belongings took over the room. All day he would sit in Father's rocking chair, swaying back and forth and chain smoking Camel cigarettes. The curtains remained closed, and the overhead light burned night and day. I wondered why my mother didn't say something. My mother made a weekly trip to the light company to make at least a token payment on our electric bill. The office supervisor had promised her that he would not cut off our lights as long as she made regular payments on the bill.

The door to the living room remained closed, and my mother ventured in only to advise Mr. Dickinson when meals were ready. About an hour before my father was due home from work, Mr. Dickinson would wash up, change clothes, and be sitting in a chair on the front porch when my father arrived. Day in and day out, the routine never varied.

As my parents were in many ways very private people, we had never had a lot of visitors. Lately, the numbers had increased because we were one of the few families on the block that still had electricity. Neighbors would come by in the evening to listen to the radio. Sometimes, the crowd would fill the living room and overflow into the dining room. My father would fix popcorn for the children, and my mother always managed to have a plate of snacks to pass around. My brother and I loved it. It was like having a party every night. After Mr. Dickinson came, the crowds decreased and finally disappeared completely. Only Uncle Smitty came by in the evening to sit on the front porch with my father and Mr. Dickinson.

My mother was a homebody. Mrs. Eubanks always said, "Miss Grace loves her home. I believe she could stay in the house forever."

That's why it was so strange when her behavior abruptly changed. Practically every evening, she would take me by the hand and walk around the corner to Aunt Bessie's house. There I would sit on the steps and look through my aunt's kaleidoscope while she and my mother engaged in deep conversation. Every now and then a word would draw my attention, but I would soon return to the wonders of photography. However, I stopped and listened when my aunt said, "Gracie, you have to do something. People are really beginning to talk. Having a white friend is one thing, but allowing a white man to live in your house when you have a young daughter is beyond the pale. It just isn't done. I think you had better talk to Smitty. I'm surprised he hasn't said something before now."

Although he came by every evening, he was not the Uncle Smitty we knew and loved. While my father and Mr. Dickinson reminisced about old times, Uncle Smitty would sit with his chair tilted back against the banister silently smoking cigarette after cigarette. About ten o'clock, regular as clockwork, he would stand up, take a deep stretch, say goodnight, and head for home. His footsteps as he passed under my window would briefly rouse me from sleep, then fade away into the distance.

When Mr. Dickinson had been at our house for close to two months, my mother and uncle began to put their heads together. They spoke in short, angry bursts of words. They were so caught up in their conversation that they forgot I was hiding in the corner, taking in every word. My uncle kept saying over and over again, "Gracie, it's time for him to go. Someone will have to tell him. People are beginning to talk. Everyone thinks highly of Bill, but if that man doesn't leave soon . . ."

His voice trailed off as if the consequences of Mr. Dickinson not leaving were too horrible to contemplate.

Before he could finish his last sentence, my mother said, "I don't know what we can do. You know how loyal William can be. He would never let a friend down. He doesn't seem to understand that anything taken to an extreme becomes a fault."

I didn't think my uncle had heard my mother, but suddenly he said, "Yes, I know how Bill is. But if he won't tell him to leave, I will!"

The following Monday, Uncle Smitty stayed home from work. He waited until my mother had left for the market before approaching Mr. Dickinson. He told Mother that he banged on the door for at least five minutes before Mr. Dickinson came to open it. He was still partly asleep and looked as if he hadn't shaved in at least four days. When he recognized my uncle, he stepped back to let him in. Uncle Smitty told my mother that he seemed to have a premonition of what was to come, because he laid down on the daybed and pulled the covers over his head. My uncle's anger was still apparent as he described the events of that morning to my mother.

"Gracie, I have never been as angry in my life," he said. "There he lay, a big slug of a white man, with everything in the world to live for, sucking the life out of a man whose shoes he isn't fit to shine. I didn't know how to begin, I was that angry!"

He finally began by telling Mr. Dickinson that he definitely had to leave. That he was ruining Bill's reputation in the neighborhood, a reputation it had taken years to create. When Mr. Dickinson tried to defend himself, my uncle lashed back at him, asking, "Why did you come here? Downtown Detroit is filled with hotels. You can afford to stay in any one of them. No, you had to come to the ghetto to wallow in self-pity. Did you think you could stay here forever? You're always talking about how Bill saved your life; you're right, he did. I don't know many men who would wrestle a man with a gun to save a friend's life. Now it's payback time. If Bill loses the respect of the people in this neighborhood, he might as well be dead."

My mother nodded her head in agreement. It was, however, his next statement that caused her to put a finger to her lips in a hush-hush gesture. My uncle was so caught up in reliving the events of the day that he did not notice. His voice rose as he said, "Do you know he tried to defend his actions by saying he would do the same thing for Bill. That Bill would be welcome in his home at any time. That's when I really blew a gasket! Welcome in your home! Maybe so. You've got enough money and prestige to get away with having a Negro stay with you for a few days. But answer me this, would you tell your friends that Bill saved your life while the two of you were riding the rails together? Would he be welcome in your home if you had a twelve-year-old daughter living there?"

By the time Father returned from work, Mr. Dickinson had been gone for some time. Father asked my mother what had happened, and she answered, "William, I don't know. He just suddenly gathered up his belongings and left. He said he'd talk to you tomorrow."

The look on my father's face was a mixture of distress and relief. When my uncle came by later in the evening, he told him about Bob's sudden departure. Uncle Smitty just smiled and said, "Perhaps he and his old lady decided to get back together. I wouldn't worry about him. He wouldn't have left unless everything was all right."

It was two days later that my father heard from Mr. Dickinson. He stopped by to thank him for his hospitality. He said everything was all right and that he and Sarah had decided to go for counseling. They had a good marriage; it just needed a little mending. My father told him how pleased he was by the news. They parted, vowing to keep in touch. It was three years before we saw Mr. Dickinson again.

It took a while for things to get back to normal. Gradually, our neighbors returned to gathering around our radio to listen to the *Lone Ranger*, the *Shadow*, and of course *Amos and Andy*. Eventually, people began to comment, openly, on Mr. Dickinson's stay at our house. Mr. Wilson summed up the general consensus when he said, "You know how Bill Sprague is. I don't know what he got out of that white man, but I bet it was a lot more than that white man got out of him."

Praise be! My father's reputation as one of the neighborhood's wise men remained intact.

THE COLOR OF COLOR

I had my first birthday party when I was thirteen years old. By today's standards it was a very modest affair, but to me it was the social event of the summer season. The only problem was who to invite. Mother had limited the party to twelve people and had left the determination of who that twelve would be up to me. Oh, how I pored over that list. It took nearly a week to pare my initial list down to just twelve. I knew that those not on the list would be disappointed, but they would just have to understand. After all, it was my party and my decision to make.

When my mother saw the final list, she smiled and passed it cross the dining room table to Aunt Bessie, saying, "I really believe Marvin is colorblind. Look whose name is on the list."

I knew from the position of her finger on the sheet that she was referring to Sylvia K. Colorblind! How could my mother say such a thing? My father had explained the race problem to me starting at a very early age. If anyone in our neighborhood knew the difference between black and white, it was my brother and I. Whenever we reported a negative experience we had suffered at the hands of a white person, Father would sit us down and say, "Don't waste time worrying about ignorant people. Remember, you're as good as anyone and better than most."

But Sylvia K. was different. Beatrice, Sylvia, and I had started kindergarten at Sill School on the same day. When we went to the playground for exercise period, Sylvia was the only white kid that would play with both black and white. Whatever her criterion was for forming friendships, it did not include color. Eventually, Beatrice and I began to see her as neither white nor black but just as Sylvia. My mother, however, did not know Sylvia. All she saw was a little blond-haired, blue-eyed, Polish girl who lived in an all white neighborhood near Michigan Avenue.

When Mother saw tears forming in my eyes, she put her arms around me and said, "Now, stop crying. We'll invite Sylvia, and perhaps she will come."

When I gave Sylvia the invitation, she seemed surprised but said nothing. I rattled on about my mother's preparations for the party, but Sylvia remained silent. We parted at the schoolyard gate to make our separate ways home. As she headed south on Thirtieth Street, I called out after her, "See you at the party."

The following Monday morning, I waited in vain by the north gate for Sylvia's arrival. When the third, and final, bell rang, I was forced to end my vigil and run to my classroom. I was surprised to see Sylvia sitting in her usual seat with her head bent over her homework. When lunchtime came, she disappeared only to reappear surrounded by a group of her white friends. She walked past me without saying a word and kept her distance for the rest of the day.

When my father learned of my disappointment at Sylvia's failure to attend the party, he said, "Baby, you might as well get it through your head right now that white folks, with few exceptions, don't want to associate with black folks. Every once in a while you will run across one who sees past color to the person beneath, but they are few and far between."

It was not until we graduated from Sill School and started Condon Junior High that Sylvia told me what had really happened. When Sylvia showed the invitation to her mother, she was initially very pleased. Then she noticed the address and asked, "Exactly where does your little friend live."

When Sylvia answered, "On the corner of Scotten Avenue and Herbert Street," all hell broke loose.

Sylvia's mother grabbed her and slapped her, hard, across the face, screaming, "How dare you bring an invitation to a nigger's party into this house."

It was Sylvia's screams that brought her father running and saved her from a severe beating. Both her mother and father forbade her to associate with me, or any other Negro child, threatening dire consequences if she did not obey.

When Sylvia finished her explanation, we vowed to remain secret friends for the rest of our lives no matter what they said. For the first time, I kept my own counsel and did not mention this conversation to my father, but I did stick with my own kind and never again attempted a close friendship with a white schoolmate.

There was, however, an even more painful side to the color question. It was the internal prejudices within the black race based on skin color. In the end, it was these prejudices that bruised my ego and reduced my self-esteem the most.

On the Saturday before Easter in 1941, Aunt Bessie came by to take me shopping. She had promised to buy my Easter shoes, and the stores on Warren Avenue would soon close. The David Green Shoe Store was our destination. Since it was quite a distance across the boulevard, we were rushing to get there before it closed. As we entered the store, we met Marie and her mother coming out, shoebox in hand. I started to introduce Aunt Bessie to Marie's mother, but since Mr. Green was already closing the blinds on the front windows, we did not stop. Mr. Green had a pair of black patent leather shoes left in my size, and we emerged breathless but satisfied.

Monday morning Marie came up to me in gym class and asked, "Was that your mother you were with Saturday?"

"No," I replied, "That was my aunt Bessie."

Before I could say another word, Mary Alice Williams spoke up and said, "Oh, no, her mother's much lighter than that. Mrs. Sprague is light enough to pass."

Mary Alice's words struck like a bullet, then whirled around and around in my head.

Everyone within a ten-block radius knew how my father felt about light-skinned Negroes who passed for white. Whenever passing was mentioned, he would say, "I don't understand why they do it. They're not only disgracing themselves, but they're deserting their families. Family is the only thing in this world that you can really count on," he would say, with an angry shrug of his shoulders.

Father's words kept bumping against Mary Alice's words in my mind. The more I thought about them, the more confused I became. There was no way to avoid it. I would have to ask my father to explain how the two sets of words could exist side by side.

After school, I rushed home. I wanted to take a good look at my mother. Maybe there was something I had missed. All these years she had been neither dark nor light, just Mama.

My mother was standing at the kitchen stove, stirring a pot of soup. The steam rising from the open pot moistened her hair and made it sparkle from the sunlight streaming through the window that overlooked the back porch. It was true! Bathed in the sunlight, Mother's skin was light. Light enough to pass for white. With the slight curl pressed from her hair, she could be any dark-haired white woman!

That evening, when Father rounded the corner of Bangor and Herbert Streets, he found me sitting on the curb waiting for him. He was not surprised, as I often met him if I had something to discuss that I did not want my mother to hear. I loved my mother, but my father was my confidant. "What's up?" he asked. "Is everything all right?"

I did not respond to his greeting but jumped up from the curb and said, "Mary Alice said Mama was light skinned enough to pass for white. You've always said that light-skinned Negroes were stuck up and arrogant. Mama is not stuck up, and she's not arrogant. I don't understand!"

Father sat me back down on the curb and sat down beside me. For a long moment, he stared into space, then said, "Marvin, maybe I didn't make it clear. Your mother is not stuck up, and she's certainly not arrogant. That's why everybody loves her. But if she were not the sweet, loving person that she is, there are people in our neighborhood who would hate her just because of the color of her skin. The light-skinned people I refer to are the ones who believe they are better than other Negroes simply because their skin is light. Those who have better opportunities because white folks see themselves reflected in their faces. Why do you think I constantly tell you that you are as good as anyone and better than most? It's because I want you and your brother to understand that who and what you are is not dependent on the color of your skin."

Over the years, I was to put my father's words to the test many times. The coloring of my skin placed me in a unique position. I was too light for dark and too dark for light. The very dark skinned called me yellow, and the very light skinned called me black. Neither fish nor fowl, I stood on the sideline and observed the havoc wrought by a condition that was simply an act of fate.

Time passed, and the civil rights movement came and went. Black was beautiful. Within the black community, the criteria for judging beauty underwent, if only temporarily, a massive change. The blunter the facial features, the darker the complexion, the more celebrated the beauty. As time and weather did their work on my complexion, I moved out of limbo into a category marked dark complexioned. Free at last! Free at last!

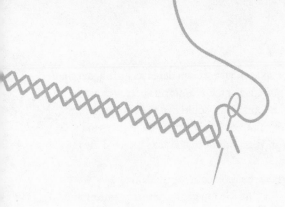

MISTER SANDMAN

James Riley was an unusual man. When he moved into the old Kennedy house, people came from near and far just to catch a glimpse of him. The albino who lived over on Bangor Street created quite a stir wherever he went, but it was nothing like the whirlwind of curiosity James Riley generated when he hit the streets. You see, he was the color of sand, that slightly reddish, golden beige sand used in the sandbox at Watson playground.

Not only was his skin sand colored, but he wore sand-colored clothes. He was never seen wearing anything other than overalls and long-sleeved work shirts that were the exact color of his skin. It was Mr. Lewis who accidentally gave him his nickname. One day he made the comment that James Riley looked like he was made out of sand. The comment was picked up and passed from person to person until it changed into Sandman and then Mister Sandman.

His appearance made him a curiosity, but it was his insistence that no one in the neighborhood, be they man, woman, chick, or child, address him by any name other than James Riley that truly set him apart. If addressed as Mr. Riley, he would not respond. It is safe to say that he received more "good mornings" from the neighborhood children than any adult in the history of the neighborhood. The thrill of not using a title when addressing an adult was an event not to be missed.

To say that Mr. Riley's—pardon me—James Riley's insistence on being addressed sans title by one and all upset the congregation of the Church of the True Believers was the understatement of the year. Grumbling was heard throughout the church. Even Reverend Elder joined in, preaching a sermon that soundly reprimanded James Riley for his conduct. She became so excited that she suggested that he might be "in league with the Devil!"

To understand why the congregation was so upset by James Riley's refusal to be addressed as Mr. Riley, you would have to examine the social structure of the

Negro society of that day. Among people who were considered as little better than animals by the white world, the importance of maintaining a strict regimen of courtesy and respect within the black community could not be overemphasized. Any adult who refused to use the title of Mr. or Mrs. reduced themselves to the level of children and weakened the grip of all authority. Titles separated the men from the boys.

Amid the tumult, it was my mother who took courage in hand and approached James Riley on the subject. She tried to get my father to go with her, but he just said, "Gracie, you should mind your own business," and went back to reading his newspaper.

She returned from her conversation shaken to the core. She freely admitted that perhaps my father had been right, and she should have minded her own business. "William," she said, "I have never been so frustrated in my life. Do you know what that Negro had the nerve to say to me? That he had come into the world James Riley, and if that name was good enough for his parents, it was good enough for him. I give up. We'll just have to explain to the children that Mr. Riley is a bit odd."

My father nodded his head yes, but I don't recall him discussing James Riley, or his oddness, with anyone.

Juanita Miller was an attractive young woman. Her skin was the color of black velvet, and her hazel eyes were flecked with gold. She was plump, but not fat, and had a head full of black wavy hair. It was when Juanita smiled that she moved from attractive to beautiful. She had the broad, open smile of a child, sweet and trusting. Juanita had never attended school, as she was considered mentally slow. The kids in the neighborhood knew that she could hold a conversation as well as anybody. We also knew that she was afraid of adults and always froze up in their presence. That is, every adult but James Riley. From the moment they laid eyes on each other, they were both obviously smitten.

The single ladies in the neighborhood were furious. Although James Riley appeared to be somewhere in his early fifties, he was still considered a prime catch. One of the single ladies was heard to say, "What can he possibly see in that simple-minded girl?"

Simple minded or not, Juanita Miller was his choice.

Aunt Bessie said, "Gracie, I never believed in love at first sight, but I do now. At least it took you and Bill a few months to decide that you were the only people in the world for each other; it must have taken Juanita and James all of two minutes."

In less than a month, James Riley asked permission of Juanita's parents to marry her. When the Millers asked Juanita if she wanted to marry him, her "yes" could be heard up and down the block. I felt a surge of excitement when told that the wedding was to be on my birthday, July 8. Nine months from the wedding date, James Riley Jr. was born, a carbon copy of the man everyone in the neighborhood referred as the Sandman.

Four more little Rileys followed with what my mother considered alarming regularity. Five years of marriage produced five children. Fortunately, the streak ended with the fifth birth. Everyone in the neighborhood drew a sigh of relief. My father was the only person who did not seem concerned. "After all," he said, "the Riley family doesn't seem to want for anything, and they live better than most of the people in the neighborhood."

James Riley's ability to support his family without resorting to welfare was grudgingly admitted by the entire neighborhood. There were those, however, who predicted future doom for the family. Mr. Wilson, who headed a three generational welfare family, solemnly predicted, "The bigger they come, the harder they fall."

None of this reached James Riley's ears since he did not visit anyone in the neighborhood. He did hold office every evening after supper at the corner of Herbert and Bangor Streets. There, he would cheerfully answer any inquiries from his neighbors. He knew everything. While it was generally acknowledged that Mr. Sprague was the wisest man in the neighborhood, it was an established fact that James Riley had more facts and figures crammed into his head than anyone who had ever lived on the west side.

Whenever my father referred to him, he would say, "There's more to James Riley than meets the eye. He's a highly educated man."

There were those in the neighborhood who believed that James Riley's past harbored some dark secret, so they were not surprised when a sleek sedan, with out-of-state license plates, stopped in front of his door one summer evening. Out stepped a light-skinned women dressed in the latest fashion. She knocked on the Riley door, and when Juanita answered, she asked to speak to James Riley.

Mrs. Lewis, the Rileys' next-door neighbor, craned her head in a vain attempt to hear what was said, but they spoke so softly she couldn't hear a word. She thought the woman called him Father, but she wasn't sure. She did see her motion to the man sitting in the car to join them. The three then entered the Riley house and closed the door behind them.

Later that evening James Riley did an unheard of thing. He came down to visit my father. They sat on the back steps and joined in a long conversation. Although I took my favorite eavesdropping position behind the window that looked out on the back porch, I heard nothing. What I did learn about the situation was pieced together from scraps of conversation overheard between my mother and Aunt Bessie. At last, I knew the secret.

James Riley had come to our neighborhood from Wilmington, Delaware, and was already married to another woman when he married Juanita. The young woman who visited him was his daughter, and the man was her fiancé. Somehow, she had found out that her father was in Detroit and had badgered his brother until he gave her the address. She wanted him to give her away at her upcoming wedding.

When James Riley disappeared for nearly a month, everyone assumed he had gone to Delaware to spend time with his other family. Only my parents knew differently. Juanita's mother came to stay with her to help with the children and to keep her company during his absence.

When James Riley reappeared, he and my father held another back porch consultation. This time, I was determined to hear, so I stationed myself beneath the steps leading up the porch. I heard more than I wanted to.

"Bill," James Riley said, "at first I didn't know what to do, but the more I've thought about it, the more I've come to believe that Juanita and I being together is right, and the life I led in Wilmington was wrong. I had an engineering degree, a good teaching job, a finer home than most Negroes, and a family that completely ignored me. I was miserable. I was trying to be someone I'm not. Here, I have a good construction job, my supervisor lets me use my engineering skills, I'm well paid, and my family respects me. I'm just James Riley, and that's all I want to be."

My father sat in silence. Finally, James Riley stood up and said, "I'm going to do what we talked about. It will be finished within the next three months. Everything should be settled by Christmas."

Father shook his hand and said, "Do what you have to do, James. Do what you have to do."

Within the next two weeks, James Riley disappeared again. With him went Juanita's dimpled smile. She was seldom seen outside her house, and when she did appear, she was a shadow of her former self. Her mother asked Mrs. Eubanks if she thought she should take her to the doctor. "No," Mrs. Eubanks replied, "there's nothing wrong with Juanita that James's return won't fix."

As usual, Mrs. Eubanks was right. When James Riley returned, the smile returned to Juanita's face and the roundness to her hips.

It was early fall when the For Sale sign went up on the Riley house. Within a week, he had received three offers. My father said, "Gracie, there's been so many improvements made on the property that it's a steal at the offering price. I really wish we could afford it, but I don't see any way."

Mother consoled my father, saying, "There'll be other houses. When the time is right, we'll find a house."

Mr. Lewis, who lived next door, purchased the Riley house. He had recently received an insurance payment from the death of his wife. He told my father, "Mathilda would be pleased with me buying the house for our son and his family. I can't think of a better use for the money."

So for two families, out of death came life. The Lewis family began the establishment of a family complex that would eventually consume most of the houses on Bangor Street between Herbert and Hancock. The Riley family ended their life in Detroit and moved to West Virginia.

After their departure, Father revealed that James Riley had spent his time away from Detroit building a new house for his family on a piece of land he owned in West Virginia.

At first, a steady stream of letters and postcards arrived from the Rileys. Gradually, the flow slowed to a trickle and then dried up completely. The last letter arrived shortly before Christmas, 1942. It contained a blurred black-and-white photograph of the Riley family standing before a large white house that appeared to be built into the side of a hill. Written across the bottom of the photograph were the words "Who and where I want to be. James Riley."

THAT LYING WONDER

As graduation day drew near, I realized that next fall I would be attending Condon Junior High. My mother had completed my graduation dress—a white linen A-line dress, with embroidered tea roses around the neckline. Aunt Bessie had brought me pink linen low-heeled pumps, and Mrs. Eubanks shopped for a matching clutch bag. I was beside myself with excitement. Then, trouble reared its ugly head. Because of the size of the school auditorium, it was decided that each graduate's family would receive only three tickets to the ceremony.

My mother anxiously counted the names of those whose attendance was considered mandatory. No matter how she figured, the bottom line remained four people and only three tickets. When she wondered aloud, "William, what should I do?" Father looked up from his newspaper in exasperation. "There isn't anything you can do, Gracie," he said.

There was, of course, my mother and father, Uncle Smitty, and Aunt Bessie to consider. Fortunately, my brother had announced early on that he had no intention of attending a grade school graduation. When the school announced they would make one additional ticket available for each graduate, but only for a member of the immediate family, I was relieved that I would not have to choose between my aunt and my uncle. It was when I expressed my relief at this turn of events that my so-called friend Ruby saw fit to inform me that Aunt Bessie was not really my aunt.

The day dragged on and on. When the final bell rang. I did not wait for my friends but rushed out, cutting through backyards and running red lights in my haste to get home. Out of breath and trembling in every limb, I ran from room to room in search of my mother. I found her on the back porch, up to her elbows in soapsuds as she scrubbed grease spots on my father's kitchen uniforms.

"What's wrong?" Mother asked, as I fought for breath to speak.

"Ruby English says Aunt Bessie is not my aunt," I replied.

"Not your aunt! Oh, I see that Lying Wonder has reared his ugly head again," she said, as she scrubbed furiously on the uniforms.

It was hard to tell if the cloud of steam that encircled her head came from the tub of hot water or from the surge of anger that obviously engulfed her.

"She may not be your blood aunt, but Bessie is your aunt because I say she is your aunt!" my mother replied, as she continued to pound the uniforms. From the look on her face, they might as well have been Ruby English.

The relief of absolute conviction flowed over me. If my mother said it was so, then it was so. The next day, she sent a note to the principal requesting an additional ticket for Marvin's aunt, Mrs. Bessie Williams. Even in the midst of all the excitement, I wondered how Ruby knew so much about my aunt. The answer to this question was not long in coming, for that Lying Wonder had already begun his devilish work.

That Lying Wonder was Mother's personal name for the entity commonly known as Satan or the Devil. I once asked her where the name came from. "Your grandmother always used it, and her mother before her. It just seemed to fit," she replied.

Coming events would demonstrate the truth of that statement.

When I received the extra ticket, I wasted no time rushing home to give it to Mother. After all, it was a special ticket for a very special lady, Aunt Bessie. It was my aunt who let me drown myself in her expensive colognes and bought endless yards of ribbon for my braids. She even told me tales of her life in Chicago, where she had met and fallen in love with Uncle Chuck.

Aunt Bessie spoke of her life as a singer working in Chicago's black nightclubs on the south side. My eyes widened as she described elegant restaurants, mammoth theaters, flashy floorshows, and all-night parties frequented by the notorious gamblers and numbers kingpins who ruled the Negro neighborhoods. She boasted that her name was still remembered along the high life circuit she had once traveled. All of that changed when she met Uncle Chuck. When he asked her to marry him and move to St. Louis, Missouri, she said yes without hesitation.

When my mother decided to leave home and seek work in St. Louis, Aunt Bessie's lifestyle change became permanent or, as my mother said, almost permanent. It seemed that while my aunt had left Chicago, Chicago had not left her.

Several of her Chicago friends kept in touch and occasionally drove down to St. Louis to visit and share the latest Chicago gossip.

When Uncle Chuck's job was moved to Detroit, Michigan, our family soon followed. My mother immediately joined the Church of the True Believers, and Aunt Bessie joined her on the march down the aisle.

Aunt Bessie was one of the most cherished members of the Church of the True Believers. There is nothing quite as delicious as being able to lay claim to a fallen woman who has been saved through the grace of God and the perseverance of a godly woman. Based on the general consensus of the congregation, my mother, who had led Sister Bessie out of a life of sin and degradation, was considered well on her way to sainthood.

Uncle Chuck worked on the railroad and was home only one weekend per month. With the typical fickleness of children, out of sight was out of mind. He was seldom seen in the neighborhood, even on his infrequent weekends home. Whenever his name was mentioned, it was in hushed tones followed by a glance, aside, to make sure the children weren't listening. We children saw him so seldom that the adults' actions did not even arouse our curiosity.

He was as fair skinned as my aunt was dark complexioned. With his thick wavy hair, hazel-colored eyes, pencil-thin mustache, and fine physique, he was an imposing figure—or so the ladies said. Father often expressed the view that Chuck had far too fine an eye for the ladies; however, it was obvious that my aunt adored him, so Father kept his own counsel. She had even asked the church to pray that they might be blessed with a baby since Uncle Chuck so desperately wanted a son.

Graduation day dawned bright and clear. Never had there been a more perfect June day. Aunt Bessie came by to give me my graduation present. She said she wanted me to have it because I might want to wear it to the ceremony. Aunt Bessie was right. It was a beautiful ladies' Bulova watch. She shyly explained that it was not a new watch, but that it did have a brand-new band. She needn't have bothered to explain, because it was my first watch and beautiful beyond belief!

After the ceremony, everyone milled about on the school lawn. Tables had been set up to hold refreshments, and a select group of fifth graders darted among the guests offering thin slices of pound cake and small cups of strawberry punch. As proud graduates, we ate as many servings as we could lay hands on, being careful to reserve room for the contents of the ice cream freezer ripening under a blanket on our back porch.

We were just about to leave when Mrs. Eubanks looked up and spotted the

English family approaching. Under her breath, she muttered, "The idea of bringing that little slut to the ceremony. She should be ashamed to show her face around here."

She was speaking of my friend Ruby's eighteen-year-old cousin, who had spent three weeks with the English family the preceding summer. Whose baby was Mrs. English carrying? The answer was not long in coming. Swinging to a sudden stop in front of my aunt, she fanned back the blanket covering the baby's face. "I know Bessie wants to see this baby. It would be a shame for her to miss seeing this beautiful baby boy," she said.

With that, she shoved the baby into my aunt's arms.

Aunt Bessie held the baby close and smiled into Mrs. English's face. "Whose baby is this?" she asked.

Ruby's mother replied with a sly smile, "Oh, it's Ramona's baby. You know, my niece that visited us last summer." Pulling a young girl forward, she said, "You remember Ramona, don't you?"

While Mrs. English had been speaking, my aunt had pushed the blanket farther away from the baby's face. Immediately, I felt the arm that touched mine begin to tremble. As I stood on tiptoes to better see the baby, an involuntary gasp escaped my lips. I saw a beautiful baby boy who looked exactly like my uncle Chuck. Only the pencil-thin mustache was missing. As I held my breath, my aunt said, "Oh, yes, I see," and handed the baby back.

On the walk home, no one mentioned the incident, but a deep pall had descended over the celebration. Aunt Bessie did not stop at our house but proceeded on home. After dishing out ice cream for the neighborhood graduates, Mother grabbed her purse and left the house. We all knew that she had gone to console my aunt.

About an hour later, Uncle Smitty came by. He and my father stepped out on the back porch and engaged in what appeared to be a very vigorous conversation. It frightened me to see my usually mild-mannered uncle pound his fist on the banister while grimacing in anger. When Uncle Chuck came up, Father did not invite him into the house, as usual, but held a terse conversation from the porch. Uncle Smitty turned his back. Finally, Uncle Chuck dropped his head and walked away.

I could hear only brief snatches of the conversation between my father and uncle after he left. In an indignant voice, Father said, "I know this is 1942, but some things never change. Why, Marvin's almost fifteen years old! I told him I don't want him in my house ever again, and I mean that!"

The next day, I rang Aunt Bessie's doorbell, but there was no answer. When I questioned my mother, all she would say was, "Your aunt is spending a few days with some friends in Chicago."

Although her tone was calm, her expression was worried.

It was not until the following Monday that Ruby brought the news that my aunt was back. Before I could finish washing the supper dishes, she returned to report that a man had been seen bringing luggage out of Aunt Bessie's house and loading it into the trunk of a long, black automobile. From the number of bags, it looked as if she would be gone for a long time.

I ran down Herbert Street to Bangor Avenue, turning left as I raced toward my aunt's house. There she was, talking to a well-dressed man, a complete stranger to me. Suddenly, I lost all control. Tears streaming, nostrils dripping, I threw myself at her, clutching her tightly around the waist and burying my face in her skirt. "Where are you going? Are you coming back? Oh, please come back, Aunt Bessie," I screamed.

My aunt held on tightly to steady herself, cupped my face in her hand, and looked down into my eyes. As I sobbed, the strange man touched her on the elbow. "Bessie, we have to go now. You know you have a ten o'clock show tonight," he said.

"I know," she responded, "but this is important. My little Marvin is important." With a deep sigh, she patted me on the shoulder. "Yes, Marvin, I'll be back. How could I ever leave you?" she said.

My aunt reached down and kissed me on the cheek. The stranger assisted her into the car, and they drove off. I stood gazing after the car until it had turned the corner and passed from view.

When I told Mother what Aunt Bessie had said, she smiled and said, "William, did you hear that? Bessie will be back."

My father looked up from his newspaper to return her smile, then resumed his reading.

After supper, my father got out the wire popcorn popper, filled two bowls with buttered popcorn, and entertained us with stories of his life on the road. Nearby, my mother happily arranged and rearranged her quilt pieces in intricate patterns as yet unnamed. Although no one mentioned my aunt, we all knew the evening was a celebration of her safe return from a place far beyond the city limits of Chicago, Illinois.

The following Sunday morning, Aunt Bessie appeared in our kitchen door at her usual time. Gone were the red satin dress, black satin pumps trimmed with sequin bows, and the pearl necklace she had worn when she left for Chicago. Her Sunday uniform of black skirt, white silk blouse, and sensible, low-heeled pumps replaced them. Only the pearl earrings remained as evidence of her battle with that Lying Wonder. I do not remember the exact Sunday that the earrings also disappeared, but they did.

ALL THINGS RELATIVE

The summer of 1942 was noteworthy for many reasons. World War II was in full flow. Rationing of food and gas had become a way of life. Many families, including mine, raised chickens in their backyards in direct contradiction of city ordinances. Whether you were ticketed or not depended on your relationship with the local police. My father was wise enough to share the wealth. He was never ticketed.

But I found the summer of 1942 noteworthy for two entirely different reasons. The continued sense of betrayal I had experienced from my favorite teacher, Miss Marjorie Reynolds, using the dreaded N word while teaching our social studies class, and the deep pain I felt when my uncle filed for a divorce from Aunt Freddie and she moved back to Chicago.

Miss Reynolds had been my friend. Although she was white, she was the first teacher who seemed to understand my dreams for the future and stood ready to encourage and assist me in obtaining them. The fact that my father liked and respected her only increased my admiration. If a race man like Father liked her, she had to be special. That made her betrayal even more unforgivable. Although I would never admit it, I did miss her.

I was still recovering from the Reynolds's affair when fate dealt a second blow, Uncle Smitty and Aunt Freddie divorced. I was my uncle's favorite niece, just as he was my favorite uncle. My aunt's primary virtue could be summed up in one sentence. This was a woman who realized that while a fourteen-year-old girl might need a new pair of shoes, what she really wanted for her birthday was a bottle of Chanel Nº 5 cologne.

The summer stretched before me—one long, seemingly endless, road. I no longer went to the Saturday matinees at the Beechwood Theater. I visited Lothrop Library so seldom that one of the librarians came by to see if I was all right. My mother assured her that I was just a little under the weather and would probably visit the library the next day. The next day came and went, and, as usual, I spent it sitting on the back steps, daydreaming of how things might have been.

I did not realize it at the time, but my parents were growing increasingly concerned about me. I was asked if I wanted to attend day camp. The summer day camp program, which was run by the state, was free to underprivileged children, although most of those attending were far from underprivileged. In fact, the camps served as political patronage for the children of precinct workers of the incumbent political party. My father had some party connections and thought he could wangle me a spot. Normally, I would have been excited by the possibility of attending day camp, but somehow the idea did not appeal. When I answered, "No, I'm not interested in going," my father really became alarmed.

Finally, he decided to play his trump card. He wrote to Aunt Freddie.

As much as I tried to sustain my sad and melancholy mood, I was excited about visiting Aunt Freddie. I would leave Detroit by train on the Thursday afternoon before my birthday and return the following Sunday evening. My mother insisted on registering me with Traveler's Aid so that I would be monitored both on leaving Detroit and arriving in Chicago. My father thought it unnecessary, but my mother said, "You know Freddie means well, but time means nothing to her."

Finally, my father grudgingly agreed, although he put his faith in several Pullman porter friends who worked the Detroit to Chicago run. He had once worked as a chef on that run. With one telephone call, he insured my safety on the trip from beginning to end.

The fact that I was visiting Aunt Freddie at all was a miracle in itself. My mother had agreed to let me go only after Father promised that one of his railroad buddies would check on me, personally, everyday. Mother had not forgotten the day that Aunt Freddie had visited us in less than pristine condition.

She finally agreed when Father asked, "Well, Gracie, do you have any other suggestions? Something has to be done."

In 1942, the south side of Chicago was something that had to be seen to be believed. The migration of Negroes from southern towns to the Windy City was in full swing. South Parkway was awash with black faces. Sidewalks were jammed with people, sometimes walking five and six abreast. The war effort was in full flower, and money was plentiful. The large ornate apartment buildings, which had once been the sole province of whites, were now filled with black families. Each building had its own personality. Some buildings were filled with recent southern migrants, while others were occupied, primarily, by established

Negro families who were a part of the ongoing black cultural renaissance. Aunt Freddie lived in such a building at the corner of Forty-third and South Parkway.

Only in Chicago could the visit of an almost fourteen-year-old niece form the basis for an elaborate party, complete with cocktails and live music. It seemed the musicians were in town to play a benefit concert and had decided to stay over for one of my aunt's famous parties. The music was loud, the partygoers were louder, and my aunt's friend Al kept the wine and whisky flowing like water.

Al was the sort of friend every woman would like to have. Absolutely besotted with Aunt Freddie, he reminded me of one of the dogs that would lay at my sister Jewel's feet in wait for the smallest caress. No matter the circumstances, Al stood ready to respond to Aunt Freddie's slightest whim.

One of the guests had brought her teenage daughter, and we entertained ourselves by hanging out of the bedroom window facing South Parkway. The hour grew late, but South Parkway was as well lit and thronged with people as if it were four o'clock in the afternoon. I thought it was because it was a Friday night, but Elnora said it was like that every night. We fell asleep on the floor under the window but awoke securely tucked into my aunt's bed.

The next day, we went shopping. We rode downtown in Al's black Packard convertible, pretending not to notice the envious stares directed our way. Our first stop was at a millinery boutique where Aunt Freddie shopped for a hat to go with a new white lace outfit she had made. As my mother made her own hats, I had never seen anyone try on hats in a shop. It was years later that my mother explained why my aunt had covered her head with a scarf before trying on hats. It seemed that if white clientele discovered that a shop allowed Negroes to put hats on their bare heads, they would no longer patronize that shop.

That evening, I experienced another first. My aunt took me to a supper club, Charlie and Eddie Mae's, for dinner and a show. The owner obviously knew my aunt well. He seated us at the rear of the room near a side door, ordered complimentary drinks for my aunt and Al, and told the waiter to bring me a large Coca-Cola. "Freddie, if you see the 'The Man' come in, you know what to do," he said, pointing to the side door. "I tip them well, but you never know," he said with a smile.

My aunt gave him a wink and then raised her glass in a salute. The house lights dimmed, the curtain rose, and the show began.

I doubt that Father would have approved of the show I saw that night. I know that Mother would not have, but I sat transfixed, hanging on to every word and gesture. Someone named Big Maybelle Brown was the star of the show. It was only when she began to sing that I recognized her as a singer on several of the records Miss Lila had given my mother, the records that Mother played only in Father's absence, when she would let the tears flow. Somehow I knew that these were private times, and although I usually told everything I knew, I kept my mouth shut.

The tap dancer did impossible steps. When he did back-to-back splits, the room exploded with applause. There was a comedian, but since I understood little of what he said, I didn't find him very funny. It was, however, the last number that brought tears to my eyes. Big Maybelle sang a medley of down-home blues to an audience that grew suddenly silent. You could hear a pin drop. Aunt Freddie said, "That woman can look into you heart and sing your pain."

When the curtain dropped, there were several seconds of silence, then wild applause. There were no encores, and the club soon emptied.

The next day was what my aunt Freddie called a sleep-in day. It didn't come a moment too soon. Never had I stayed up so late and slept so little. It was beginning to catch up with me.

Later that afternoon, we dressed to go out as my aunt said there was something she wanted me to see. On the way, Al stopped by Charlie and Eddie Mae's to return some glasses my aunt had borrowed for the party. It didn't look like the same restaurant. In the cold light of day, every layer of dirt stood out in bold relief. The lights over the small stage were on. What had appeared last night to be glitter dancing under the changing colored lights, today proved to be miniature swirls of dust blown by the ceiling fans. Aunt Freddie just smiled. "Looks a whole lot different in the daylight, doesn't it?" she said. I could only nod my head in agreement.

Al drove downtown and let us out in front of a theater plastered with large posters of ladies in various stages of undress. As he opened the door to let us out, he looked at my aunt with a puzzled expression on his face. "Are you sure you want to do this, Freddie?" he said. "Yes, I'm positive," she replied. After a long pause, Al closed the car door and drove off.

At the box office, my aunt asked to see the manager. When he came, he seemed overjoyed to see Aunt Freddie. While I stood on the sideline, they held an agitated conversation, which resulted in his finally saying, "Well, okay, Freddie, but you'll have to sit on the side in the back of the theater. I don't want any trouble."

That was how I came to see my first, and last, burlesque show.

It was midafternoon, and the theater was barely a third full. As my eyes adjusted to the darkness, I looked at the people around me. They were mostly middle-aged men. Some were slumped in their seats, half asleep, while others were clapping loudly and shouting, "show time."

Finally, the tattered curtains opened to reveal a man dressed as a clown and clutching a standup microphone. The audience seemed to know him and began to chant, "Bugsby, Bugsby, Bugsby."

He immediately began telling what seemed to be jokes, although he spoke so fast they didn't make sense to me. The audience, however, laughed uproariously, and my aunt studied my face for my reaction. When I leaned back and briefly stared off into space, she smiled and patted my hand. Finally, Bugsby finished his act and left the stage, followed by a trickle of applause. Then, the act the audience had been waiting for came on.

My eyes widened as a line of chorus girls took to the stage and began to dance wildly, arms flailing and legs lifting and lowering, in an imitation of the French cancan. I stared and stared. What stories I would have to tell! Gradually, my interest waned as I began to see the patches in the faded costumes and the rings of perspiration under the armpits and around the necklines.

As the chorus girls waved their legs, they revealed the numerous runs that laddered their rayon stocking. Finally, I recognized the acrid odor that filled the theater. It was the same odor that my father and uncle had when they returned from a weekend of hunting or fishing. An odor created by too much physical activity and too little soap and water. Suddenly, I lost all interest in the show and longed only to escape to the open air of the Chicago skyline. "Are you ready to leave, Baby?" Aunt Freddie asked. My answer was to rise and hurriedly leave the theater.

My first action after arriving home was to run a hot bath, loaded with bath salts, and soak until my aunt came to the bathroom door to ask if I had shriveled up and washed down the drain.

For supper that evening, we went across to the hotdog stand and bought franks and fries, which we ate sitting on the small balcony overlooking South Parkway. The night was warm and still, and gradually I forgot the events of the day as Aunt Freddie and I gossiped and giggled together like two young girls.

The next day was Sunday and time to go home. At the train station I clung to Aunt Freddie until she forcibly removed my hands and put me on the train. All the way home, I thought of the things I had seen—the slim skyscrapers, the elegant shops, the hordes of people, but most of all Charlie and Eddie Mae's and the burlesque theater. I wished I could tell Miss Reynolds about my experiences, because she more than anyone would understand how firmly the events of this trip had cemented my determination to become a writer, a recorder of those small, commonly shared experiences that make us more alike than unlike.

My father and uncle met me at Union Station. On the ride home, I described my experiences in Chicago. Both urged me not to mention my visits to Charlie and Eddie Mae's or the burlesque theater. "Your mother wouldn't understand," they said.

Then, as if he had just remembered, Father reached into his jacket pocket and handed me an envelope. In it was a birthday card from Miss Reynolds.

Wonder of wonders! All was forgiven! I could hardly wait to get home and write her a letter. I had so much to share. I would ask forgiveness for not understanding and tell her all about my experiences in Chicago. The words were already taking shape in my mind!

On arriving home, I gave my mother and brother a hurried greeting, grabbed paper and pencil, and curled up in the window seat in my parents' bedroom to write this epic letter. On into the evening I wrote, the words pouring forth effortlessly. Never before had my thoughts formed in such a logical manner. I was inspired. The letter seemed to write itself. I completed it at dusk, just as the streetlights came on. My mother found me a blank envelope, and I sat down to address it, while Father searched for a stamp in his wallet. It was at this moment that joy turned to deepest despair. The front of the envelope had only two entries, my name and address, and a postmark of Boulder, Colorado. There was not a return address in sight.

Father did not remind me of his prophecy that I would one day regret my stubbornness; instead, he made every effort to secure Miss Reynolds's address. He even visited my grade school principal, Mrs. Pringle, in hopes that she might have the address. All for naught. Miss Reynolds had disappeared into the dark hole called Boulder, Colorado. Nearly a year later, during the week of my graduation from junior high school, I received a letter from Miss Reynolds. Then nothing more.

THE GATHERING STORM

Immediately before a major weather disturbance, there is often a lull before the storm.

Skies are blue and cloud free, winds subside, and stillness descends upon the land. A sense of well-being permeates the air, and even infants still their cries. Early summer of 1943 was such a time. Peace prevailed, and by June of that year, my hair problem was finally resolved.

I cannot remember the exact moment my hair became the most important thing in my life, but it must have been shortly before my graduation from Sill School in the summer of 1942. My hair had always been the bane of my mother's existence. No matter what she did to it, it always looked the same—rough and ragged. Part of the problem was that my mother was blessed with a full head of silky, wavy hair and didn't have the slightest idea what to do with mine. She attempted to console me by saying, "Your hair will grow. By the time you're grownup, you'll have a head full of hair."

My mother did not seem to understand that the question was not so much one of quantity but of quality. Every lady of color desired long, silky hair. If you weren't born with it, then a good hard press and curl was the next best thing.

It was my aunt who took matters in hand. One Saturday morning, she marched me around the corner to the Pettway Beauty Parlor on West Warren. It had just opened and was the first black-owned business on that stretch of Warren Avenue. In less than an hour, Aunt Bessie had negotiated an agreement with Miss Pettway that swapped my father's services as a carpenter for a year of free hairdos for me.

From the very beginning, my hair responded to Miss Pettway's touch. Throughout the balance of 1942, and into the spring of 1943, it grew by leaps and bounds. By June 1943, I had a head of hair that any mother could be proud of. My mother was beside herself with joy. Every once in a while she would pat my hair and say, "Answered prayer! Answered prayer!"

My year at Condon Junior High was nearly over. Graduation was fast approaching. Next fall I would attend Northwestern High School. Although WWII was still raging, it was rumored that it would soon be over and our boys would be returning home. It was summertime, and the living was easy. There were few, if any, who noticed the storm clouds gathering on the horizon.

Sunday, June 20, 1943, was a bright, sun-filled day without a cloud in sight. The weather report on the radio said it would be another in a long series of ninety plus days. As I dressed for church, I could hear my mother pounding a piece of round steak for our customary Sunday breakfast of steak, gravy, and hot biscuits with a side of my mother's homemade peach preserves. The early birds were already gathering in front of the Church of the True Believers—the better to show off their Sunday finery. Uncle Smitty had promised to come by after church to take Beatrice and I for a ride in his new car. Church services couldn't be over fast enough.

True to his word, my uncle was waiting when church let out. When we saw his new bright red convertible, our eyes almost popped out of our heads. Up and down familiar streets we sailed, waving to everyone we passed. Horn blasting and radio blaring, on we rode. As we crossed Warren Avenue and headed toward Milford Street, the traffic became more and more congested. My uncle pulled the car over to the curb, jumped out, grabbed a man by the arm, and asked, "What's happened? What's going on?"

The man jerked away from my uncle and shouted over his shoulder, "Man, where have you been? Some white folks threw a Negro woman and her baby into the Detroit River off Belle Isle, and there's been rioting every since."

Uncle Smitty jumped back into the car, gunned his engine, and forcibly opened an avenue of escape. Once back across Warren Avenue, traffic opened up and he headed for home. Beatrice and I huddled in our seats, too frightened to move. I clawed at my face in a frantic effort to remove whatever was covering my eyes. It was my hair. The pins holding it in place had given way and the force of the wind moving over the lowered convertible top blew my hair up, out, and around my face like a halo. I breathed a sigh of relief. How could there be anything seriously wrong on a day that found my hair finally blowing in the wind? I was soon to learn how swiftly triumph could change to disaster.

The story about whites throwing a Negro woman and her baby off the Belle Isle Bridge later proved to be false, but on Sunday, June 20, 1943, it was accepted as truth, and the disturbance swiftly spread to the mainland. When an equally false rumor circulated among whites that blacks had raped a white woman, the rioting accelerated. Blacks attacked whites who were unlucky enough to be caught in their neighborhoods, and whites attacked blacks who were caught in the Woodward Avenue corridor. The rioting continued, unabated, while law enforcement fought in vain to contain the situation.

Our neighborhood hunkered down for the night. My father sat in a chair by the front door with his hunting rifle across his knees. All streetlights were out, and if there were lights on inside any of the houses, they were not visible from the street. Before dark fell, my father went to check on Beatrice and her brothers and sisters. Finding them alone and frightened, he brought them back to our house. He was still cursing as he led them in.

Although my father tried to send my mother to bed, she must have spent the night at the dining room table, because each time I awoke, I could see her silhouette through the open bedroom door. All during the evening hours, the sound of breaking glass, running feet, and pistol shots could be heard. The sky to the east was bright with flames. A cloud of smoke hung over the city, and the acrid odor of burning rubber was everywhere. Shortly before midnight, there was a faint knock at the door. When my father challenged, "Who's there?" a soft voice answered, "It's me, Mr. Sprague."

My father opened the door, and Mrs. Eubanks tumbled into the front room. When she said, "I just came to see if you were all right," both my mother and father burst out laughing.

That is how we passed the first night of the 1943 Detroit race riot.

With daylight came courage. At first light, the neighborhood began to unfurl. Doors and windows were cracked, and "good mornings" were passed across porches. Some hardy souls even ventured into the street, edging their way, gingerly, toward the corner of Scotten Avenue and Herbert Street for a quick look toward Warren Avenue. They returned to report seeing scores of people milling in the street and police cars, with sirens screaming and emergency lights flashing, threading their way among them. Above the sirens, the sound of breaking glass could be heard.

Later that evening, federal troops were called in to take control of the situation. With the arrival of the battle-dressed soldiers, some manning combat tanks and others patrolling in jeeps with their weapons at the ready, an uneasy order was restored.

The soldiers brought not only order but also courage. On Tuesday, June 22, 1943, more and more people ventured out to survey the damage. Broken glass from smashed store windows was everywhere. Light poles had been uprooted, and the charred remains of cars that had been overturned and burned littered the streets. As far as the eye could see, there was evidence of the violence that had consumed the city.

On Warren Avenue, only one white business, the Roosevelt Drug Store, had escaped damage. The pharmacist, Dr. Cole, had never refused to fill any prescription, with or without money. Grateful residents formed a human wall around his building and dared anyone to breach it.

When the smoke cleared, thirty-four people were dead—twenty-five blacks, nine whites—and property damage totaled in the millions of dollars. On July 9, 1943, the last federal troop left the area, leaving a quiet but divided city.

A NEW DAY

In the aftermath of the riot, people gathered in small groups to debate the circumstances that might have sparked it. Some thought that Negroes were tired of being treated as second-class citizens while their sons fought and died on foreign soil in defense of their homeland. Others thought it was the results of the mollycoddling of young hoodlums who refused to work and spent their days sleeping and their nights roaming the streets. It was my mother who had the last word. Never raising her eyes from her crocheting, she said, "I never thought I would see the day that I would be glad Bill Jr. was fighting in Italy, but this is that day. I believe he's safer there than on the streets of Detroit."

While the adults argued the reasons for the riot, the graduating class of Condon Junior High turned their thoughts to the burning question: When would the graduation be held?

The original June date had long since passed. If the ceremony were held on the fifteenth, what shoes would I wear? I had put linen pumps in layaway at Mary Ann's Shoe Store and placed an order to have them dyed to match my graduation dress. Aunt Bessie had given me the money to get the shoes out on the Saturday before the riot. I just had to have those shoes!

On the morning of the tenth, I gathered up several library books and asked Mother if I could return them to the library. At first, she said no, but then she changed her mind. As if conferring with herself, she said, "Perhaps it would be good for you to get away from all this for awhile. The library is one of the few places they didn't damage. Don't stay too long. Go straight there, and come straight home."

I walked slowly down Herbert Street to Bangor. As soon as I turned the corner and was out of my mother's sight, I picked up speed. When I reached my aunt's house, I slipped down the driveway and shoved the books into the milk chute on the side of the house. I raced to the streetcar stop at Warren and the boulevard just as a crosstown streetcar pulled up.

The conductor opened the door and said, "Where in the world did you come from? Where do you think you're going? I don't even know what I'm doing out here. I don't know what your parents are thinking of letting you run around by yourself today!"

Before he could stop talking and possibly close the door, I jumped aboard. I burst into tears as I began to tell him about the graduation, my pale green linen dress, and the matching shoes that I just had to have.

When I had calmed down enough to make him understand the situation, he smiled and said, "Well, little lady, I'll give you an A for spunk. Graduation is important. We may not get through, but let's give it a try."

I will never forget that ride. For most of the trip, we were the only streetcar in sight. The driver knew how to work the overhead cables to switch the car from one line to another. By the time we arrived at our destination, we had traveled halfway across the city. The driver let me off at the corner of Grand River and State Street. As I stepped down, he said, "Hurry up and get your shoes, and I'll wait here and take you back."

I ran down Grand River to Woodward Avenue. Soldiers were positioned on each side of the street with weapons drawn. Two large army tanks occupied the street adjacent to Hudson's Department Store. The south end of Woodward Avenue was cordoned off, and mounted police patrolled the barricades.

Mary Ann's Shoe Store looked as though a tornado had hit it. Broken glass covered the floor like a carpet, and empty shoeboxes were everywhere. When the old man sweeping the floor looked up and saw me, he dropped his broom and said, "My God, where did you come from? Is anybody with you? Come in! Come in out of that doorway!"

When I handed him my claim slip, he said, "I guess you really want these shoes. I don't know if they're still here or not. They took just about everything. What they didn't take, they damaged, but I'll take a look."

He was gone for about five minutes. I could hear him moving things around in the back room. Finally, he emerged holding a shoebox triumphantly aloft. Wonder of wonders, it contained my shoes. He seemed as pleased as I was. I handed him my money, and he reached down and placed a pair of nylon hose in the shoebox, saying, "Congratulations on your graduation. You might as well have these. They'll just be thrown out. Now get on home!"

I arrived back at the corner of West Warren and the boulevard to be greeted by what appeared to be half of the neighborhood. It seemed that Mary Alice Williams had sounded the alarm when she reported that the library would be closed until the following week. Most of the neighborhood fanned out to search for me. Their fears eased, but their anger increased when someone mentioned seeing a young girl, fitting my description, boarding an empty crosstown streetcar.

Followed by the crowd, I stumbled home where an even larger crowd had gathered in anticipation of seeing me get the thrashing of my life. When I saw the expression on my mother's face, I began to shake, uncontrollably. Father had to physically restrain her from leaping on me and tearing me to bits. I closed my eyes in silent acceptance of my fate, when suddenly I heard my uncle's voice above the noise of the crowd. With a chuckle he said, "Well, you've got to give Marvin credit. She is a determined young lady."

As if on signal, other voices joined in, "She sure is. I've always told Sister Sprague that nobody's going to pull the wool over Marvin's eyes."

My uncle had saved the day. He did, however, draw me aside the next day to warn me that if I ever pulled a stunt like that again, he would personally take me over his knees and whip my behind till it roped like okra. I think my mother and father welcomed any excuse not to punish me. They could see in my eyes that I had been punished enough.

Graduation day dawned bright and clear. The temperature remained in the low nineties, but the humidity had decreased, giving the illusion of a sharp drop in temperature. It was as though the frenzy of the riot had washed the air clean.

The ceremony went off without a hitch. I did as my aunt had told me and walked with my head up and my eyes focused straight ahead. After the program was over, everyone milled around outside the school taking pictures and receiving compliments from family and friends. As usual, the races were divided, with the blacks occupying the south side of the lawn, and the whites the north side. We might mix in the classrooms, but once we exited the building, we went our separate ways.

Uncle Smitty drove Beatrice and me home. He drove slowly, for the entire neighborhood had gathered on their porches and steps to watch the graduates return from the ceremony. There was much waving and calling out of congratulations, for the success of every child belonged to everyone. Finally, my uncle said, "I guess it's time to take you young ladies home. The ladies have prepared quite a celebration for you."

My celebration had begun the day before. The morning mail brought two letters. The first was from my brother in the form of a v-mail. As usual, the letter made little sense. During the v-mail process, the letters from soldiers overseas were photographically reduced in size and abundantly censured. The result was letters that had dates, times, and any other information that might give aid and comfort to the enemy blocked out. Fortunately, the most important part of the letter could not be censored. The very fact that my brother had taken time in the middle of a raging war to write me, sent a message all its own. I knew that he loved me and was thinking of me.

It was the second letter, however, that made my heart beat faster. It was from Miss Reynolds. My father thought I would be disappointed because it did not have a return address, but I was too happy to hear from her to worry about a little thing like that. Already, I had read it so many times that the folds were beginning to split. I slept with it under my pillow that night, and on my way to graduation, I could feel the pressure as it shifted back and forth under the strap of my newly acquired bra. Miss Reynolds had remembered my graduation, and that was good enough for me.

Halfway through the letter, Miss Reynolds quoted my favorite poem, "Pippa Passes." It was a poem that we had learned for our verse-speaking concert. If I closed my eyes, I could almost hear her voice repeating the words aloud. Somehow I knew that as long as I knew that poem, I would never be without Miss Reynolds.

On the way home, I asked my uncle to let Beatrice and me off at the corner of Herbert and Bangor Streets. As we started down Herbert Street, we saw Mrs. Eubanks come down her steps and head toward my house. We quickened our steps in anticipation of the celebration my mother had been preparing all week. Mother would be sitting in the old ladder-backed chair that Father had made for her. Next to her would be the picnic bench covered with one of her lace tablecloths. The bench would be laden with desserts, a caramel cake, my favorite; a lemon meringue pie for my father; several large pound cakes for the ladies from the church, who would surely stop by; and a chocolate fudge cake, just in case.

The White Mountain ice cream freezer, filled with peach ice cream, would be standing at the base of the elm tree covered with an old blanket to keep the ice from melting and to help in the ripening process. Chairs borrowed from neighbors would be scattered all over the yard. Probably Mother Blevins and Mrs. English were already in residence, sitting upright in their chairs, ankles neatly crossed, holding their tissue-wrapped graduation gifts tightly in their hands. All that was needed to begin the festivities were the graduation girls.

The party would last until every bite of dessert was consumed, and the ice cream freezer was emptied, washed, and packed away. With everyone's stomach on overload, my mother's celebration dinner would be stored in the icebox to be eaten the next day.

The summer sat before me like a prize package waiting to be opened. In a few short months, my life would undergo drastic changes.

Mr. Dickinson would reenter our lives to be reconciled with my father and forgiven by my uncle.

My brother would find safe harbor from the battlefields of Italy. He would be assigned to teach English to illiterate army soldiers who couldn't recognize their names if they saw them in boxcar letters. Everyone but my mother seemed surprised by the turn of events. Her only comment was, "Answered prayer! Answered prayer!"

Early in August, my mother would finally realize her dream, a house of our own.

In September, I would enter Northwestern High School, traveling to it from an address as yet unknown. I would leave behind the west side area that had provided me sanctuary for most of my life. I would take with me memories of the people and places that had helped to shape my personality.

Within a few short months, Beatrice would disappear, traveling to Chicago to live with her oldest sister, who had recently married. It would be ten years before I would see her again.

The heat wave would end, as heat waves always do, leaving behind a city broken in spirit but not in hope.

But all of this lay hidden behind a door marked the Future. For today, the last lines of my favorite poem applied-"God's in his heaven/All's right with the world."

As Beatrice and I strolled toward my house, we stopped, and as if responding to a secret command, locked arms, and began to run.

We ran all the way home.

Epilogue

In the days following September 11, numerous drive-by shootings, church burnings, date rapes, crack-addicted babies, high school massacres, and vicious child abuse, I often think of the people who celebrated my graduation from Condon Junior High that warm summer day in 1943. Although most have been dead for many years, their impact on my life lives on: Aunt Bessie, who was my second mother; Uncle Smitty, who treated me as a daughter and later in life finally had a daughter of his own; William, who was all that a brother should be; Jewel, whose name was true; Mrs. Eubanks, who gave me the gift of unconditional love; Miss Pleasant, who taught me the importance of giving thanks in all things, large and small; Beatrice, a true friend; Reverend Elder, who demonstrated that a woman could be both strong and feminine; Reverend Saxon, who taught me that people are not always what they appear to be; Mr. Levi and Miss Lillian, who demonstrated that true love can overcome all obstacles; Miss Lila, who proved that a little love was better than no love at all; the Harmon family, who served as my how-not-to guide when life delivered a "special" child into my keeping; Miss Marjorie Reynolds, who taught me to be careful in judging the actions of others; Aunt Freddie, who demonstrated what grace and poise are all about; James Riley, who taught me to be who and what I wanted to be; my mother and father, who were the strong threads that held the pieces together; my children, grandchildren, and great-grandchildren, the most precious pieces of my crazy quilt; and the many others who may be absent from the pages of this book but not from the recesses of my heart.

It was the strength and determination they demonstrated in life that showed me the way to rise above the birth of a "special" child, widowhood at a young age, job losses, poverty, loneliness, and prejudice to arrive, finally, at the safe harbor of old age.

From the bottom of my heart, I salute you all, and in the words of Miss Pleasant, I thank you "a hundred, million, trillion times!"

In the American Lives series

Pieces from Life's Crazy Quilt
by Marvin V. Arnett

Local Wonders: Seasons in the Bohemian Alps
by Ted Kooser

Thoughts from a Queen-Sized Bed
by Mimi Schwartz

In the Shadow of Memory
by Floyd Skloot

Phantom Limb
by Janet Sternburg

JEFFERSON PUBLIC LIBRARY
321 W. Main Street
Jefferson, WI 53549
920-674-7733

921 ARN   JUN 0 3
Arnett, Marvin V., 1928-
Pieces from life's crazy

JEFFERSON PUBLIC LIBRARY
321 S. Main Street
Jefferson, WI 53549
920 .674-7733